Ian Buxton

101 Whiskies to Try Before You Die

Also by Ian Buxton:

The Enduring Legacy of Dewar's

Glenglassaugh: A Distillery Reborn

101 World Whiskies to Try Before You Die

*101 Legendary Whiskies You're Dying to Try
But (Possibly) Never Will*

101 Gins to Try Before You Die

Ian Buxton

101 Whiskies to Try Before You Die

Third Edition

HEADLINE

Revised and Updated Edition published by HEADLINE PUBLISHING
GROUP in 2016.

First published in 2010
by HACHETTE SCOTLAND, an imprint of HACHETTE UK
2

Cataloguing in Publication Data is available from the British Library

978 1 4722 4247 1

Designed by Lynn Carr

Printed and bound in Portugal by Printer Portuguesa

Hachette Scotland's policy is to use papers that are natural, renewable
and recyclable products and made from wood grown in sustainable
forests. The logging and manufacturing processes are expected to
conform to the environmental regulations of the country of origin.

HEADLINE PUBLISHING GROUP
An Hachette UK Company
Carmelite House
50 Victoria Embankment
London EC4Y 0DZ

www.headline.co.uk
www.hachette.co.uk

Contents

Introduction

101 Whiskies to Try Before You Die is a whisky list with a difference.

It is not an awards list.

It is not a list of the 101 'best' whiskies in the world.

It is simply, as it says in the title, a guide to 101 whiskies that enthusiasts really should seek out and try – love them or hate them – to complete their whisky education. What's more, it's practical and realistic.

101 Whiskies to Try Before You Die does not contain obscure single-cask bottlings that sold out weeks before publication and it doesn't contain hugely expensive whiskies that virtually no one can afford to buy anyway (even if they could find them). After all, what's the point? I might look terrifically smart recommending, say, the Glenglassaugh 40 Years Old that won the International Wine & Spirit Competition's special trophy for 40-year-old Scotch whisky. By one token at least, that makes it the very best single malt Scotch you can buy. A panel of really well-informed and expert judges (not just one person, and not me) picked it from its peers. Though little known, it is very, very good and I could be seen to be doing you a favour by pointing you its way. But it's £1,500 a bottle. Or perhaps Glenfiddich's 50 Years Old, a snip at £10,000. Are you really going to nip out and buy a bottle? I don't think so. So I set myself some rules when I started writing this book.

Essentially, they can be summed up as: every whisky listed here must be a) generally available (although you might have to look a little bit, every one of these whiskies should be available from a decent whisky specialist or through an online retailer) and b) affordable (read on to see what that means). And, though it goes without saying, there must be a reason for their inclusion. Mostly it's because they're very, very good examples of their kind, but sometimes they deserve your support for other reasons. Sometimes it will be because they are made by small distillers swimming against a tide of corporate ubiquity, but it might just be because a particular whisky is simply so unusual that you just have to try it. That might mean reminding you of something familiar that you knew about but had, sort of, forgotten; hopefully, more often, it will point you to something new, unexpected and surprising.

Above all, this book is about whiskies to *drink*, not collect.

So I've excluded one-off bottlings or single-cask releases, because there's simply not enough to go around. And I've simply ignored whiskies that seem to me to be designed primarily for collectors. Perhaps more importantly, I've taken a very hard-headed look at retail prices. I've been highly selective once a whisky rises above £100 in a typical British whisky shop; very critical indeed if it costs £500 or more, and flatly ignored it once the price breaks the £1,000 barrier. So, sorry The Macallan 57 Years Old Finest Cut, in your Lalique crystal decanter; goodbye Dalmore 62 Years Old; and farewell to Ardbeg's ritzy Double Barrel. Tasty though you may be, your fantasy price tags rule you out. Let's get real: this book is for whisky drinkers, not Russian plutocrats.

What's more, because I don't believe in the simplistic and reductionist notion of the 'world's best whisky', everything's in alphabetical order.

And even more unusually, nothing has a 'score'. Again, I simply don't believe that you should follow one person's individual preferences and more or less idiosyncratic scoring system (and that's all that most tasting books are). There are several reasons why I believe 100-point scoring systems don't work, not least the idea that any one individual can consistently and reliably differentiate between a whisky scoring 92 and one scoring 93. It seems to me palpably absurd, so we're not going there.

Better, in fact, to take some advice from Aeneas MacDonald, the original sage of whisky, who in 1930 suggested that the discerning drinker learn to judge whisky with 'his mother-wit, his nose and his palate to guide him'. Sound words.

But so many whiskies, so little time. With the world of whisky expanding almost daily, an experienced guide may be of some value, if only to point you in new directions and suggest some unexplored and rewarding byways that you may not have considered. Scotch, American, Irish, Japanese and Canadian whiskies are all in here. As are some from Sweden and other unexpected producing nations. So I have strenuously attempted to be wide-ranging in my approach and, so far as I am able, to include some whiskies that I personally don't particularly care for but which are regarded as exemplars of their kind.

So how, you may ask, did I assemble this list?

There is no one answer.

First, I used my own knowledge and judgement. I have worked in the whisky industry for more than 20 years; consulted for a number of distillers; been Marketing Director for one of Scotland's leading single malt whiskies; created and run the World Whiskies Conference; written widely about whisky; and sat on a number of competition judging panels. So, though I still reckon I'm learning about whisky and there's something new to discover almost daily, I'm privileged to have tried a lot of different whiskies and reckon to know something about them and the people who made them.

Secondly, I looked at what my peers think. Mainly I've looked at the major award winners at important competitions such as the International Wine & Spirit Competition (IWSC); the San Francisco World Spirits Competition; *Whisky Magazine*'s World Whiskies Awards (I'm on the judging panel for that one occasionally); and more informal awards such as that from the Malt Maniacs. Tasting notes by luminaries such as F. Paul Pacult and those appearing in various international whisky magazines have all served to draw different whiskies to my attention.

And finally, I asked some of my whisky friends and colleagues to nominate their favourites – in the case of practising distillers, they had to nominate at least one of their competitors' whiskies for every one of their own, and the same rules on cost and availability were applied. Those who helped are listed in the acknowledgements page – many thanks to them. But I should explain that I used my whisky friends rather like the ancient Greeks used the Oracles – I've listened to the advice, but the final choices were mine. So blame me if you don't agree with the list.

As I write this, there are, entirely coincidentally, 101 whisky distilleries operating in the UK where I live (yes, there are at least two outside Scotland), but such is the constantly changing nature of this industry that the number will be wrong by the time you read this. Around the world there are – oh, I don't know, perhaps two hundred or so. Probably more.

And they keep opening. One of the exciting things about the whisky industry in the last ten years has been the proliferation of new distilleries across the world, especially boutique craft distilleries in 'new' whisky-producing countries. Many have excellent and informative visitor centres, but opening hours and seasons vary. Because of that, I haven't given specific details, but suggest you check online or phone in advance to confirm when they are open.

We can now get whisky from Scotland, Ireland, Canada, the USA, Japan, India, Sweden, Belgium, Switzerland, Australia, France, Austria, the Czech Republic, England, Wales, Finland, Germany, Holland, Russia, New Zealand, Pakistan, Turkey, South Korea and South Africa. Apparently, there are even whisky distilleries in Brazil, Nepal, Uruguay and Venezuela. Inevitably, more than half the whiskies in this book are single malts from Scotland, with Scottish blends and grains taking the total from my home country to an impressive 65 whiskies. But, reflecting the growing popularity, influence and quality of 'world whiskies', more than a quarter of those I have selected are from the USA, Japan and other countries – and I can assure you that you'll be impressed.

So, when you consider that all of these countries can produce any number of 'single malt' expressions differentiated by age, cask type, finish and so forth, and most of them do, and then add blended whiskies and indigenous non-Scotch styles, such as bourbon, rye and so on, to the potential universe, you can see that tasting them represents a lifetime of unremitting toil.

One of the lessons of this book is that you don't have to spend a lot of money to find really great or interesting whiskies. In fact, I didn't really look at price until after completing the list. The price ranges indicated in the text are based on the typical UK retail price from a specialist independent whisky shop, and were correct as we went to press. Around half are under £50. If you dropped the three most expensive, the rest would average around £60 a bottle – go compare that with the world's best-known wines. Whisky can be a serious bargain!

Here's the key to the 1 to 5 scale:
1 Under £25 2 £25–39 3 £40–69 4 £70–150 5 Over £150

Of course, prices change all the time. In particular, tax and duty rates change, products are put on promotion or, generally less favourably for the consumer, 'repositioned', as the marketing folks would have it. Prices will also vary if you are reading this thousands of miles away from me, in a place where costs may be higher for long-distance imports, but less for local bottles.

High rates of taxation in the UK come as a constant surprise to visitors from many countries, however, who regularly ask, 'Why is whisky more expensive here in Scotland than in my home?' For the answer, apply to the government who, at the time of writing, take around three-quarters of the retail price of a bottle of standard Scotch whisky in excise duty and VAT.

There are several thousand whiskies out there – perhaps even ten thousand. No one really knows. So, as the old joke would have it, it's tough work but someone has to do it. I've picked 101 for you to enjoy, saving you hours of joyless labour. You don't have to thank me; buying the book will do just fine.

Each one has an entry describing the whisky and the producer, with some background information that I hope you'll find useful and interesting. Then there are brief tasting notes. These are not intended to be the be-all-and-end-all, more a jumping-off point for your own exploration and to help explain why each whisky made the cut. You'll also find a space to record your own purchases, personal favourites and tasting notes.

You can catch up with my news and views on the ever-changing world of whiskies by following me on Twitter @101Whiskies.

I hope to hear from you there.

Meanwhile, sláinte!

Foreword to Third Edition

This book first appeared in September 2010 and a 'Revised and Updated' edition was published in 2013, when whisky appeared to have entered a kind of golden age unparalleled since the expansion of Scotch whisky distilling in the last years of the nineteenth century.

Since then there has been much economic turbulence, resulting in disruptive change. The emerging markets that held such glittering promise have stalled. New world distillers have convincingly demonstrated that the old order held no monopoly on quality or consumer engagement. The last of the 'whisky loch' has been drained, leading to the querulously debated creation of 'no age statement' (NAS) whiskies and, as supplies tightened, tending to force retail prices ever higher.

Yet the creativity of the industry in responding to these challenges has, if anything, been more than matched by the ardour of whisky drinkers the world over who have continued their love affair with the *cratur*, though not without maintaining a trenchant commentary on social media.

As old favourites have disappeared from shelves their replacements have been embraced with enthusiasm and so a revision of this little book is already overdue. In the course of bringing it up to date around two-thirds of the entries have either been revised or replaced entirely, such has been the pace, extent and change in the world of whisky. The price banding in the Introduction (page 10) has been maintained for consistency but the individual entries amended to reflect current pricing.

That has generally meant an increase, sometimes so substantial that it has caused me to drop a whisky entirely. But if you are not looking to find whisky for 'investment' or as a collectable, and can resist the siren lures of the fashionable brands, there are still bargains to be found and great whisky to be enjoyed and drunk.

If I have pointed out just one or two that were previously unknown to you I hope to have performed a useful service. If you aim to track down all 101, why not stop at 100 – who knows, you might live forever! Good luck, it's too late for me.

Ian Buxton

1	**Producer**	John Dewar & Sons Ltd
	Distillery	Aberfeldy, Perthshire
	Visitor Centre	Yes
	Availability	Widespread international availability
	Price	▪▪▪▪

www.dewars.com

Aberfeldy

21 Years Old

It's a great shame this isn't more widely known because I'm willing to guess that people who 'don't like whisky' would like this and people who know and like whisky would like it a lot.

The Dewar's distillery at Aberfeldy was built from 1896–98 by the restless, innovative and entrepreneurial Dewar brothers, Tommy and John, who hired Charles Cree Doig, the finest distillery architect who ever lived, to design it for them. But, for years, under the ownership of the old Distillers Company Ltd, all of the output went for blending and the single malt boom passed Aberfeldy by.

However, in one of the periodic convulsive reorganisations that the Scotch whisky industry indulges in to keep bankers and lawyers in expensive German motor cars, in March 1998 ownership was transferred to Bacardi who, up until then, had only had a minor interest in whisky. The result was a wave of investment, including what has been described by *Whisky Magazine* as 'the ultimate Scotch whisky visitor centre' and some exciting new products.

The best of these is this 21 Years Old single malt. Aberfeldy is noted for a gentle, heather-honey sweetness and this whisky is just delightful: well-mannered, delicate and surprisingly complex. It's a shame about the rather squat and ugly bottle but don't let that put you off.

It may be easier to find the 12 Years Old version – that's good, but this is a lot better and well worth the additional money. The extra age really rounds out and deepens this whisky, the subtlety of which would tragically get lost in a blending vat.

If you ever get to the distillery there is also an excellent range of exclusive single-cask bottlings.

Colour Warm gold and amber.

Nose A creamy, honeyed nose with dried fruits, heather flowers and hints of coconut.

Taste Intense but not cloying sweetness, dark orange marmalade, vanilla and oak wood. Mouth-coating and creamy.

Finish This is long, quite spicy and has hints of lemon. Restrained and elegant.

Verdict

2

Producer	Chivas Brothers Ltd
Distillery	Aberlour, Speyside
Visitor Centre	Yes
Availability	Specialists, better supermarkets and duty free
Price	■■■

www.aberlour.com

Aberlour
a'bunadh

A cask-strength whisky has quietly been making a name for itself over the past few years and has now attracted quite a crowd of enthusiastic devotees who praise the big, rich flavours of this Speyside malt.

Aberlour distillery was established in 1879 and then remodelled by the leading distillery architect Charles Doig some twenty years later after a disastrous fire. It really came into its own after 1975 when it was acquired by the French group Pernod Ricard and became their lead single malt brand in the days before their purchase of the Seagram distilleries (The Glenlivet in particular). Today the distillery offers an excellent 'Aberlour Distillery Experience' which is well worth making the effort to take (booking essential).

There are several easily accessible expressions, and the possibility of bottling your own direct from a single cask at the distillery, but the one to go for is the strangely named a'bunadh (it's pronounced a-boon-ah and means 'the origin' in Gaelic). It is non-chill filtered and at full-cask strength, the idea behind the product being to replicate a nineteenth-century-style whisky matured exclusively in Spanish oak oloroso sherry butts. So, if you like traditional Macallan or Glenfarclas, you're going to love this.

Note that this is released in batches, some of which have been criticised as tasting slightly sulphured (an effect of cask treatment), so if you find a batch that you particularly like, it might be an idea to snap up several bottles before it runs out. Equally, it's fun to keep experimenting and, perhaps, taste one batch against another. And this shouldn't be a problem, because, for whisky of this quality and strength (it's usually around the 60% abv mark), it's quite a bargain. Expect to pay around £50 for the most recent batch. The following tasting notes broadly describe the style, though each batch naturally varies.

Colour Rich and dark.

Nose A marked sherry character, possibly honey and dark fruits.

Taste Can be drunk at full strength but develops with water. Big, mouth filling, Christmas cake, dried fruits, possibly some citrus and chocolate notes.

Finish Expect a drawn-out finish, perhaps with evolving spices, oak and some smoky notes.

Verdict

3

Producer	Aldi Stores Ltd
Distillery	n/a – this is a blend
Visitor Centre	No - lots of shops though
Availability	Aldi UK stores
Price	

www.aldi.co.uk

Aldi

Highland Black 8

Though it might be a bit of a shock (alright, it's definitely a shock) to find a supermarket own-label blend here, trust me, this is a good thing. Don't ignore the bargains under your nose I'd say, and at under £15 this is definitely a bargain.

A good few years ago, when the industry was dumping excess stocks from the infamous whisky loch, there were some fabulous buys to be found amongst supermarket cheapies. Then things tightened up, prices began to rise and cheaper and younger whiskies found their way onto the own-label shelves. The proportion of malt in the blend dropped. Generally speaking, the whiskies simply weren't as good. The distillers had more profitable things to do with their stocks and a few simply stopped supplying supermarkets. Own-label became a dirty word.

Well, not this. This represents remarkable value, especially if you decant it into another bottle. That's not to suggest you pass it off as something more expensive (heaven forbid; your friends deserve better treatment than that petty deception) but a number of tasters have observed that it's better for a little air. If you can't do that, then at least give it a few minutes in the glass to let the initial rather harsh aromas disperse and you will be pleasantly surprised by the result.

Aldi have won major awards for this but I can go back to my own notes when I tasted it blind for a major consumer magazine against a number of well-known brands. It was the top blend that day and I see that my notes have it as 'sophisticated', 'balanced', 'smooth', and 'creamy'. You can't say fairer than that.

If you simply can't bear the idea of the neighbours seeing you in Aldi (what are *they* doing there, you might well ask) then other top tips from the multiple grocers include the 12 Years Old Highland Single Malt from the good old Co-op and Waitrose's 12 Years Old Islay Single Malt. They have perfectly respectable bags, so off you trot.

Colour Warm yellow.
Nose Initially superglue – but be patient, it gets better.
Taste Honey, fresh fruits, apple pie. Surprisingly smooth. See comments above.
Finish Malted fruit loaf. Disperses quickly but at the price who's worried?

Verdict

4

Producer	Amrut Distilleries Ltd
Distillery	Amrut, Bangalore, India
Visitor Centre	No
Availability	Specialists
Price	■■■

www.amrutwhisky.com

Amrut
Fusion

Indian whisky? Some mistake, surely? Well, no. India is a huge whisky market and a giant producer but the vast majority of Indian whisky is made from molasses – and so far as the EU is concerned that means it's rum and can't be sold as 'whisky'.

This is currently the basis of a major and long-running trade dispute, with the Scotch whisky industry claiming that Indian import duties are an illegal restraint of trade, and the Indian producers crying foul and pointing out that much of their distilling industry was set up by the British in the first place. Today, the Indian industry is dominated by United Spirits, producers of such fine brands as Bagpiper and McDowells. Ironically, however, following a byzantine series of transactions it is effectively a subsidiary of Diageo. But the Indian whisky that has made it into this list is actually distilled by their smaller independent rival Amrut Distilleries Ltd, established in 1948. According to Indian mythology, when the Gods and the Rakshasas (demons) churned the oceans using the mountain Meru, a golden pot called the Amrut sprang out containing the Elixir of Life.

Amrut is real single malt whisky; that is to say, it is made simply with malted barley, water and yeast, so it can be sold in the UK. And that's our good fortune, because it's really very good (you didn't think it was here just out of curiosity, did you?).

Fusion is an unusual product, unique in that it combines Indian barley from the Himalayas with peated malt from Scotland and is bottled at a healthy 50% abv. And despite that (and despite having come halfway round the world), it's pretty good value at a typical £50 a bottle. Just try not to think of the carbon footprint if you're drinking it in Tannochbrae!

Colour Bright gold. Indian whisky matures faster than Scotch, so spends less time in the cask.

Nose A pronounced wood impact, but also peat, vanilla and fruit.

Taste Surprisingly complex and engaging, the peat mixes with oak, fruit, chocolate and caramel shortcake.

Finish Yes, you will finish this and want to find another bottle. Fades to a dry spiciness.

Verdict

5

Producer	Inver House Distillers Ltd
Distillery	Knockdhu, Knock, nr Keith, Speyside
Visitor Centre	No – visits by appointment
Availability	Specialists and online
Price	■■■■

www.ancnoc.com

anCnoc
18 Years Old

You have to think that Inver House have made life unnecessarily hard by rebranding Knockdhu as the strange and unpronounceable anCnoc, Gaelic for 'the hill'. This bestowed upon the whisky the unenviable distinction of no longer being named after the distillery that produces it, but it was apparently done to avoid confusion with Knockando.

It seems a shame, because there is much to commend the Speyside single malts from this little-known distillery between Keith and Banff; in particular, its resolutely traditional style of operation (something of a signature with Inver House). An old-fashioned, cast-iron mash tun is still used, while wooden washbacks made from Douglas fir are favoured over modern stainless steel. More importantly, tradition is also proudly maintained by the continued use of a worm tub, one of just thirteen still in operation across all of Scotland, helping to give anCnoc its depth, body and characteristic rich, meaty aroma.

A mild curiosity about the distillery is that it housed troops from the Indian army during World War 2, along with their mules and horses. Apparently, the local residents would turn out to watch cavalry practice – what the riders thought of this is not recorded!

The 16-year-old version that I previously recommended has given way to this older whisky. Launched in 2014, it has been matured in a combination of European oak ex-sherry and American oak ex-bourbon casks, and bottled at 46% abv without chill-filtration or additional colouring (quite right too). The benefits of the two additional years in cask are apparent in the greater weight and darker colour, adding to the mouthfeel and body of the whisky. If you're looking for smoke, then stay away – this is all about distillery character and cask aging, with no peat influence to mask the underlying spirit.

Though the price has increased it's still not excessively expensive when compared to other 18-year-old whiskies.

Colour Rich gold.
Nose Slightly medicinal; lemon zest; fresh fruits; vanilla takes over.
Taste Brown sugar; orange zest; rich and quite full bodied.
Finish Holds together well, with the sherry-cask influence apparent to the end.

Verdict

6

Producer	Glenmorangie plc
Distillery	Ardbeg, Islay
Visitor Centre	Yes
Availability	Widespread international availability
Price	▪▪▪

www.ardbeg.com

Ardbeg
10 Years Old

I can't really make my mind up about Ardbeg. I love the place, admire what's been done there and acknowledge the legions of passionate fans who have supported this iconic Islay distillery since it reopened in 1997. It also has the best food of any distillery visitor centre I can call to mind.

But I also feel it's overly pleased with itself. Personally, I find the faux 'homespun' tone of much of their promotion grates with me, especially as it could be said to imply that this is some tiny independent struggling for survival against ruthless corporate giants, when in fact it's owned by one of the biggest luxury goods companies on the planet (Louis Vuitton Moët Hennessy). And don't get me started on the ludicrous 'luxury' nonsense which is Ardbeg's £10,000 Double Barrel. It's simply absurd.

However, there's no denying that the current team have done an excellent job, and Ardbeg does produce some deeply loved whiskies, as long as you like them peaty. This is arguably the benchmark Islay whisky, against which all others must be judged, and for that, we'll forgive it a lot.

The standard is the 'entry-level' 10-year-old expression which critics have raved about. The stills at Ardbeg differ from others on Islay, being taller and having a curious purifier on the spirit still, the combination of which contributes to the finesse and delicacy of what is a very highly peated spirit. Certainly this is truly complex whisky and, love it or hate it, you just have to explore its finer, non-chilled nuances at least once.

And, sorry, but I simply have to mention the distillery's Kiln Cafe once again. It's worth a trip just for their lovely grub.

Colour A pale, straw-coloured whisky, set off by the elegant, tall, green glass bottle.

Nose Monstrously peaty, of course, but with attractive citrus notes; cinnamon and pears.

Taste The initial attack of the peat slowly gives way to cereal and barley notes; tobacco, coffee, liquorice and chocolate.

Finish Smoky and slightly sweet; hints of barley linger and you may find some vanilla notes.

Verdict

7

Producer	Morrison Bowmore Distillers
Distillery	Auchentoshan, Dalmuir, nr Glasgow
Visitor Centre	Yes
Availability	Widespread international availability
Price	☐

www.auchentoshan.co.uk

Auchentoshan
Classic

It seems only right to include one example of distilling in the true, traditional Lowland style – that is to say, triple distilled, like Irish whiskey. Auchentoshan is also a showpiece distillery, beautifully maintained by its owners Morrison Bowmore (now a subsidiary of the Japanese group BeamSuntory) and thus always a pleasure to visit.

The distillery was established around 1817 in open countryside, since which time residential development has surrounded the plant and it now appears a curious anachronism in an apparently urban setting close to the dramatic Erskine Bridge over the River Clyde. The owners have capitalised on this location by opening not just a visitor centre but also providing conference facilities for the business market.

The range of whiskies has been greatly increased in recent years and a number of different expressions, right up to 50 years old, are offered. It is light and delicate in style but, surprisingly, stands up well to cask finishing when this is handled with due sensitivity – the Three Wood is a fine example of what can be done and Auchentoshan seems to age quite gracefully. Presumably this reflects shrewd cask selection by the previous owners and continued investment by BeamSuntory.

The result of Auchentoshan's triple distilling process is a smooth and very clean spirit that finishes life at over 80% abv, unusually high for the output of a pot still. There is an admirably clear animated diagram illustrating this on the excellent website – itself a model of clarity and unfussy operation.

If you don't know this whisky, then I suggest you start with Classic. It's non-aged and the soft, creamy style will win friends easily. If you don't care for it, or find that you want more body, don't despair – its gentle style makes an excellent base for whisky cocktails, providing grip without dominating the desired flavour.

Colour Pale and delicate – bottled quite young and matured in refill ex-bourbon, this hasn't picked up much colour.

Nose Loads of vanilla; fresh and grassy.

Taste Malty, plenty of marzipan sweetness cut with lemon zest and green apples.

Finish Fresh and floral, but doesn't linger.

Verdict

8

Producer
Distillery

Visitor Centre
Availability
Price

Bakery Hill
Bakery Hill Distillery,
North Bayswater, Victoria
No
Specialists
■■■■

www.bakeryhilldistillery.com.au

Bakery Hill
Classic Malt

'I come from a land down under
Where beer does flow and men chunder'

Remember the 1980s smash hit 'Down Under' from Men At Work?
Bet you can now! Australia's craft distilling revolution brought it to mind.

Bakery Hill's Classic Malt comes at 46% abv and cask strength.
The latter is somewhat assertive for my tastes, but they can be
rightly proud of what the distillery has achieved, especially as they
only began operations in 2000. At 16 years a classic single malt
Scotch might just be getting into its stride: the Bakery Hill malts
are striking for their maturity and complex development.

A few bottles made it to the UK, but lately they've been in short
supply. Turns out the reason is that their own home market has
discovered that these whiskies are – for the most part – really
rather good. With limited production there's only so much whisky
to go around and naturally the domestic market has taken priority.
So perhaps 20 years ago the beer did flowing as Men At Work
reminded us, but now Australians have developed a real taste for
the true amber nectar.

Now, as you read on, you'll see that the industry has begun to
develop a view that Scotch is a luxury good that has been
underpriced for years. I daresay they're right, but I do fear that,
sooner or later, this is going to end badly as rising prices meet
consumer resistance.

And that is all the opportunity world producers, such as the
ambitious Aussies, the super Swedes of Mackmyra and the
tenacious Taiwanese of Kavalan, will need to jump in and fulfil the
global market that Scotch has conveniently opened up.

Right now, Bakery Hill can't fulfil anything more than a tiny share
of the demand. But they're growing and there are several more
Australian distilleries in action, all working flat out. So it may be
early days for world whisky producers but Scotch distillers might
want to spin that Men At Work hit onto the next lines.

Colour Light gold.
Nose Cold mulled cider.
Taste Honey dribbled onto fresh baking. Warm muesli and
apple puree.
Finish Smooth and spicy.

Verdict

9

Producer	Inver House Distillers Ltd
Distillery	Balblair, Edderton, Ross-shire
Visitor Centre	Yes
Availability	Specialists
Price	◼◼◼

www.balblair.com

Balblair
Vintage 1999

Balblair is just along the road from its much better-known neighbour Glenmorangie (see separate entry) but maintains an altogether lower profile, perhaps rather grudgingly. The distillery is one of a clutch owned and resurrected by the Airdrie-based Inver House Distillers, themselves a subsidiary of the Thai conglomerate InterBev, who seem to specialise in taking other companies' unloved orphan children and making something of them.

It is one of the oldest distilleries still in existence in Scotland, dating back to 1790, though there are records of distilleries on the site as far back as 1749. It was rebuilt in the 1870s by the owners, the Ross family (four out of the nine Balblair distillery workers still have the surname Ross), and appears to have changed relatively little since then, although it was shut from 1915 to 1947. Inver House aren't easily persuaded of the merits of change and tend to adhere to traditional methods where they can.

What is not particularly traditional is the decision to release a series of vintage expressions, rather than the more normal aged variants. However, vintages have worked very well for Glenrothes and there is some merit in the argument that spirit character does vary from year to year. It all adds variety to our shelves and has definitely worked in sales terms.

Previously, I'd listed the 1989 vintage but as that is getting scarce and has broken through the £100 ceiling I suggest we move on. Like the earlier release, this represents a happy compromise between availability, price and quality: it embodies the distillery style well, yet remains affordable and immensely quaffable. For more modest budgets the 2003 and 2005 releases are also available.

Colour Beaten copper.
Nose Aromas of raisin, green apple and hints of pain au raisin.
Taste Initially lightweight, but rapidly evolves and warms, as the sherry cask impact comes through. A rich fruit cake with delicate spice, citrus fruits and vanilla.
Finish Some dried fruit, but finishes quite quickly. Hints of smoke and a marine note.

Verdict

10

Producer	Balcones Distilling Inc
Distillery	Balcones, Waco, Texas
Visitor Centre	Tours by appointment
Availability	Specialists
Price	◼◼◼

www.balconesdistilling.com

BALCONES

BABY BLUE
made from roasted blue corn

750 ml   CORN WHISKY   46% alc./vol.

THE ORIGINAL TEXAS WHISKY

Balcones
Baby Blue

For a while there in 2013, Balcones was probably the hottest thing on the micro-distilling scene, beloved of bloggers and rapidly developing a cult following amongst whisky's chattering classes, who fell over themselves to heap praise on Balcones' single-minded and innovative products.

But 'pride comes before a fall', or 'walk before you can run' or some such similarly sententious sentiment springs to mind. Not long after that, everything imploded: distillery founder Chip Tate had a spectacularly acrimonious public falling out with his financial backers and left to set up again on his own. Presumably he and his avid fans assumed Balcones would then fold ignominiously.

Far from it: 'no one is irreplaceable' (more pursed-lip moralising there for you) and life carried on under Head Distiller Jared Himstedt who, in fairness, had been with Balcones since its inception. In fact, things got better (well, larger) as the distillery moved to a new 65,000-square-foot site in downtown Waco – just up the road from their original distillery location – with some shiny new stills from Forsyths.

Today Balcones has four core products: Texas No. 1 Single Malt, Brimstone, Baby Blue and Rumble, plus limited editions and special releases. According to Himstedt, 'Good drink is a beautiful thing, and in a world that could use a bit more joy and beauty, we feel honoured to get to do this for a living.' Ah. How nice.

Baby Blue was their first product and, in fact, the first legally distilled whisky in Texas since Prohibition. It's also the only whisky (yes, they spell it the British way) made from Hopi blue corn. It's certainly an appealing drop: I asked my wife to try some and she reacted as follows: 'That's whisky with all the unpleasant bits taken out.' As all the unpleasantness at Balcones is behind them and all is now sweet harmony, you can't really say fairer than that.

Colour Mid-amber with copper tones.
Nose Citrus, vanilla, popcorn and honey.
Taste Sweet, with a hint of fire. Amaretto liqueur and tropical fruit.
Finish Mrs Buxton says, 'I would sit and drink that with pleasure.'

Verdict

11

Producer	Chivas Brothers Ltd
Distillery	n/a – this is a blend
Visitor Centre	No
Availability	Specialists and duty free
Price	■■■

www.ballantines.com

Ballantine's

17 Years Old

This is a whisky with a considerable and distinguished pedigree, largely unappreciated in its home market. This, for a brand that markets itself with the slogan 'leave an impression', is more than slightly ironic. It's because this is a premium blend which, by and large, is a style that the UK market doesn't 'get'. Not that the owners, Chivas Brothers, will be especially bothered because Ballantine's is huge in the Far East and in tax-free outlets (airports, to you and me).

The name is an honoured one. The original George Ballantine was one of the giants of Victorian whisky blending, starting from modest premises in Edinburgh in 1827 but, less than 60 years later, exporting around the world with a string of royal warrants to his name. However, as is the way of the spirits industry, the brand changed hands several times before Chivas Brothers acquired it in July 2005.

Between their astute marketing and the skills of their renowned Master Blender, Sandy Hyslop, Ballantine's has come roaring back. Fortunately, Hyslop has a very fine range of both grain and single malt whiskies from which to pick, and the experience and judgement to know how to put them together.

Probably the pick of the bunch is the 17 Years Old. It is pleasant, smooth, warming and mellow. There's plenty of depth there, but this does not assert itself forcefully; rather it slowly charms you until you realise what a very special dram it is.

Talented but self-effacing and modest with it: the archetypal upper-middle-class Edinburgh professional, then. It does leave an impression, after all.

Colour Bright gold.
Nose Rounded, balanced and appetising. Some sweet notes and a hint of smoke.
Taste Mellow vanilla tones, with maturity showing in balanced wood, smoke and cream. Surprisingly full bodied for 43% abv and after chill filtration.
Finish Lingers agreeably at the back of the palate, holding together well and leaving hints of marine character.

Verdict

12

Producer Chivas Brothers Ltd
Distillery n/a – this is a blend
Visitor Centre No
Availability Specialists
Price ■■

www.ballantines.com

Ballantine's
Christmas Reserve

Once a year – around Christmas, if you haven't guessed – the folks at Ballantine's bring out a special limited edition. And very fine, and very remarkable value it is.

Last year it typically retailed at £28. I tasted it blind with an audience at the Speyside Whisky Festival and asked them to guess the price – around £40 was the average, with several higher bids. Bear in mind that these were, by definition, quite knowledgeable whisky enthusiasts – no one went below the retail price, which perhaps is all you need to know.

It's another Sandy Hyslop creation, with the aim of recreating and bottling the flavours of Christmas. So you'd expect more of a noticeable sherry-cask influence, with lovely nuts, rich fruit cake and dark chocolate orange – and you wouldn't be disappointed. They're all there, but wonderfully balanced and superbly poised.

Though supplies are necessarily limited and there is no guarantee that an edition will be released every year, it's been a consistent seasonal presence since 2010 and I for one hope for a re-appearance as reliable as a Slade soundtrack in a supermarket.

Now, the smart drinker, recognising the limited nature of this release, will lay in a few bottles to see them through the dark, cold rainy days of a British summer but strangely, if you look carefully, you may find the odd retailer who takes the description literally and starts to discount their stock once the festive season has passed. Without too much effort I found bottles available (at the time of writing – July) for £23, and that's just silly.

So let's be clear – a dog is not just for Christmas and neither is this whisky. Look out for one in your stocking and make sure Santa keeps his hands off it.

Incidentally, with the price, and the weight, body and flavour of this whisky, it makes a great cocktail base.

Colour Burnt amber.
Nose Fruit cake, apples and pears. Freshly cracked nuts.
Taste Nuts, rich fruit cake, dark chocolate orange all in abundance. It's a cracker in fact!
Finish Ginger, caramel and spices. All is peace, harmony and goodwill to all men.

Verdict

13

Producer
Distillery
Visitor Centre

Availability

Price

William Grant & Sons Distillers Ltd
Balvenie, Dufftown, Banffshire
Yes – but booking in advance
is necessary
Specialists and possibly some
better supermarkets
■■■■

www.thebalvenie.com

The Balvenie

PortWood 21 Years Old

The Balvenie is the little brother to Glenfiddich and, for some years, has been rather unfairly overshadowed by its stablemate (almost literally, as it happens, as the distillery lies just below the Glenfiddich site).

More recently, however, Grants have understood the quality offered by The Balvenie and promoted it more actively with a growing range of releases. The distillery is characterised by maintaining a floor malting, one of the last in Scotland, and may be acquitted of the charge of keeping this on solely for its tourist value by the fact that, until even more recently, it was closed to the public.

However, you can now take an excellent tour which, though superficially expensive, in fact offers great insight into production at The Balvenie and culminates with an extensive tasting of older whiskies, making it very good value. Numbers are limited so it is essential to book in advance. Concentrating on the whisky, the usual clichéd audio-visual presentation is absent (which only enhances the pleasure).

There are a range of expressions and styles but my favourite is the 21-year-old PortWood finish. Some of these finishes can be overdone and the whisky spoiled by an unsubtle use of the second wood, but this was created by the hand of a master. Delicate port wine flavours dance round the inherent spirit quality in a mesmerising and quite beguiling fashion.

David Stewart, Grants' Master Blender, has spent longer than he probably cares to admit in the industry and is widely respected by his peers. For me, this is a stellar achievement, fully justifying his high reputation.

Colour Warm highlights in rich gold.
Nose Raisins and nuts; continues to develop a well-rounded sweetness over time.
Taste Silky and full bodied, the port casks seduce but never swamp the underlying spirit character.
Finish Lingers very nicely and continues to offer a well-mannered, nutty memory.

Verdict

14

Producer	William Grant & Sons Distillers Ltd
Distillery	Balvenie, Dufftown, Banffshire
Visitor Centre	Yes – but booking in advance is necessary
Availability	Specialists
Price	■■■■■

www.thebalvenie.com

The Balvenie

Tun 1509

Are there really 1500 tuns (vats) at the Balvenie distillery? It's a big place, I know, but that seems a lot. Never mind, you just need to know that this is another very fine product from Balvenie's David Stewart.

I know that these Tun range Balvenies are expensive, but they're not the top of the range. For that you need to find nearly £30,000 for a bottle of the 50 Years Old. You could buy a very nice Audi or BMW for that money, and being honest most of us would take the motor. The good news is that you can have your smart new wheels and still enjoy one of these.

The series started out life as a limited distillery-only release. Subsequent batches have been produced for different markets, such is the demand for this legendary dram. Tun 1401 has given way to this expression which, at the time of writing, is enjoying its ever-popular third release – there are around 9,000 bottles available. If you can't find one don't despair as there will surely be further releases.

To be technical for a moment, 31 casks went into this: 12 sherry butts distilled between 1989 and 1992, 11 American oak hogsheads distilled in 1989 and eight refill American oak butts distilled in 1992 and 1993. So, it's non-aged but there's loads of information on the packaging.

Now, something about David Stewart, who was recently awarded an MBE for services to whisky. After nearly 55 years in the employment of William Grant & Sons, this gentle, thoughtful man is approaching retirement (when he can spend more time watching his beloved Ayr United). Though Grants will retain his expertise as a consultant he will be hard to replace, and a very hard act to follow. Drink to his health.

Colour Warm, mellow copper.
Nose Intense, complex and fragrant.
Taste Barley sugar sweetness, gentle spices (ginger and cinnamon to the fore), some oak and lovely mature dried fruits. The sherry-cask influence is wonderfully balanced with honey and soft vanilla.
Finish Honey, wood and spice with lingering vanilla.

Verdict

15

Producer	BeamSuntory
Distillery	Jim Beam, Clermont Distillery, Kentucky
Visitor Centre	Yes
Availability	Specialists and online
Price	▢▢

ARTFULLY AGED

BASIL HAYDEN'S
Kentucky Straight
Bourbon Whiskey

WHEN BASIL HAYDEN, SR. began distilling his smooth BOURBON here in 1796, KENTUCKY was but four years old and GEORGE WASHINGTON was PRESIDENT.

Today, we make BASIL HAYDEN'S Kentucky Straight Bourbon WHISKEY using the same skill and care that made it a favorite among AMERICA'S frontier settlers.

DISTILLED AND BOTTLED BY
KENTUCKY SPRINGS DISTILLING CO.
CLERMONT · FRANKFORT, KENTUCKY USA

750 ML   40% ALC./VOL. (80 PROOF)

www.basilhaydens.com

Basil Hayden's

It's claimed that the Hayden family can be traced back to the years following the Norman Conquest of 1066. One ancestor, Simon de Heydon (sic), was knighted by Richard the Lionheart in the Holy Land during the Third Crusade in the 1190s and his son, Thomas de Heydon, made Justice Itinerant of Norfolk by Henry III. Later, another ancestor was granted a large estate in Hertfordshire, in return for the family's military service. Eventually, however, they emigrated to the Virginia Colony in the 1660s in search of religious freedom. I can't see that any of this matters, other than to cloak an all-American product in a certain 'old world' gentility. Still...

It is further claimed that, by 1796, one Basil Hayden was a master distiller, born and raised in Maryland, where he learned to make whiskey from rye. Moving to Kentucky, Hayden began making whiskey from a base of corn, but added a higher percentage of rye than other distillers, resulting in smooth, mild bourbon. Well, that's the story anyway. PR folk love this sort of thing.

One of the Beam Small Batch bourbons, Basil Hayden's is unique in that it utilises twice as much rye (30 per cent) as other Small Batch releases (though Beam adopt a similar approach to the distillation of their Old Grand-Dad). Unusually for premium bourbon, it is bottled at 40% abv, typically at around eight years of age, and is the lightest in style in the collection.

It always seems somewhat over-packaged for my taste with a tall and rather feminine bottle strangely bisected by a copper band, but if you like a dry and more delicate taste in your bourbon then this will appeal. It's also an excellent cocktail base.

Like all the Small Batch range, this comes from the large and rather utilitarian Clermont distillery, somewhat the antithesis of the small batch philosophy, but where you can at least visit the T. Jeremiah Beam Home and the Jim Beam American Outpost and try a range of products.

Colour Pale gold.
Nose Some citrus notes with mint and spice.
Taste Light to medium body, delicate and aromatic. Honey, pepper and fading spice.
Finish Quite short but holds together.

Verdict

16

Producer	Brown-Forman Corporation
Distillery	BenRiach, Elgin, Morayshire
Visitor Centre	No – try phoning for an appointment
Availability	Specialists
Price	▢▢

www.benriachdistillery.co.uk

BenRiach
Curiositas Peated

Bored of whiskies with strange Gaelic names? Why not try one with some Latin, part of a range that includes Herodotus Fumosus and Importanticus Fumosus? You just have to be curious about 'Curiositas'. (It's an experimental, heavily peated Speysider.)

The names may seem a bit contrived, but here is a small independent distiller (well, they were when I first wrote this, but read on) getting on with life, experimenting with unusual whiskies and managing to do so without developing a persecution complex.

BenRiach (I have no idea why they stick a capital letter in the middle) was lying mothballed from around 1900 until it was rebuilt and reopened sixty-five years later. It's a miracle it survived, but it only carried on until August 2002, when it was mothballed again.

However, at that point, its luck changed. Having been owned by a series of large corporations, BenRiach was acquired by industry veteran Billy Walker, backed by two South African investors. They invested heavily and, in August 2008, bought Glendronach as well, so things were obviously going swimmingly. And, since then, things have obviously gone very well indeed as US distilling giant Brown-Forman has moved in to buy the whole company.

Sadly, there's no visitor centre (though there is an excellent one at Glendronach), but they have restored the showpiece floor malting and so it might be worth asking ever so nicely for a wee peek.

There are a number of releases, some quite limited, and exciting plans. The distillery themselves say that their vision is 'not only to maintain the great traditions of the distillery but to break new ground with "*new*" whisky expressions and, borrowing from the wider world of the noble art of distilling, to "*craft*" special whiskies, and 'intriguing expressions'. It sounds exciting. It is exciting. And, hoping that the corporate giants don't swamp them, my toast to BenRiach is '*Nil carborundum illegitimi!*'

Colour Pale gold.

Nose Peat on this one, but not as aggressive as often found on Islay. Heather flowers in background.

Taste Medium weight, lots of peat attack, wood follows on with a spicy fruitiness.

Finish Plenty of that peat smoke but lots more going on to tease you *a capite ad calcem.**

Verdict

* '*From head to heel*', since you had to ask. Were you asleep in Double Latin?

17

Producer
Distillery

Visitor Centre
Availability
Price

Gordon & MacPhail
Benromach, Forres,
Morayshire
Yes
Specialists
■■

www.benromach.com

Benromach

Organic

There are a number of 'organic' whiskies out there – Da Mhile (first made at Springbank, but now Loch Lomond); Highland Harvest blended and Bruichladdich's 'The Organic'.

Personally, I can't see that it matters all that much in a distilled spirit, but if you care about these things, you will be interested in this offering from Benromach, Gordon & MacPhail's tiny distillery on the outskirts of Forres. So far as I can see, it was the first whisky where the whole process – raw ingredients, distillation, maturation and bottling – was certified to Soil Association standards. So well done, Gordon & MacPhail.

This does, however, add something of interest to the whisky enthusiast. For one thing, the barley used for malting comes from a Scottish farm (not all barley used to make Scotch is Scottish, which may come as something of a surprise) and the barrels are from virgin oak. This is unusual – it's generally held that brand new oak barrels exert too assertive an influence on the flavour of Scotch whisky, hence the almost universal presence of barrels that have been seasoned by previous use. However, Benromach appear to have carried this off and, while clearly evident, the wood does not dominate.

The distillers claim that the casks are 'hand selected' – a nice-sounding but, as far as I can see, essentially meaningless claim, since so far as I am aware, no one has yet invented a machine to select casks – and made from natural, wild-growing forest. The trees are not sprayed with pesticides or any other form of chemical prior to felling (but then they wouldn't, being 'wild') or indeed after.

Quite how you square your green concerns with the felling of natural wild forest is a matter for your own conscience, of course. You'll probably drink this while reading the *Grauniad*.

Colour Rich, deep gold.
Nose Lots of wood impact, of course, but fruits and vanilla pods.
Taste Wood we take for granted here, but fruit compote and some sweetness also evident.
Finish A glow of liberal, green-tinted virtue.

Verdict

18

Producer	Heaven Hill Distilleries, Inc.
Distillery	Bernheim, Louisville, Kentucky
Visitor Centre	Yes
Availability	Specialists
Price	▪▪▪

www.bernheimwheatwhiskey.com see also www.heavenhill.com

Bernheim
Original Wheat Whiskey

'Unique' and 'original' are grossly over-used terms, though I think probably justified here. This American whiskey is made with winter wheat as its principal ingredient (a minimum of 51%) along with the more conventional rye, barley and corn. As such, it is the first really new American whiskey since Prohibition and is arguably reviving a distilling style from the 1700s. Naturally, as the world's only straight wheat whiskey, it has attracted a lot of attention from enthusiasts anxious for a new taste sensation. At time of writing it is one of the very few examples of this style, though presumably, if its success continues, we'll see other distillers offering something similar in the near future.

The distillery itself has had an interesting history. It was built on the site of the old Astor and Belmont distilleries, which were demolished by United Distillers, the forerunner of Diageo, before the brand new Bernheim plant was constructed in 1992. Under Diageo, bourbon was not regarded as a priority and, in 1999, the Heaven Hill Company acquired the facility, which today makes it the last privately owned distillery in Kentucky.

Among other brands, Heaven Hill Bourbon and Rittenhouse Rye are distilled here, all of which can be seen in the fine new Bourbon Heritage Centre, *Whisky Magazine*'s 2009 Visitor Attraction of the Year (there is a $50 'behind the scenes' tour). Bernheim Original is distilled here but aged for a minimum of two years in new charred white oak barrels in Rickhouse Y at Heaven Hill's site at Bardstown, Nelson County.

Launched in 2005, Bernheim Original Wheat Whiskey has benefited from interest in small batch production and craft distillation. As an innovative salute to tradition it is interesting but the whiskey itself holds up well.

Colour Pale, especially by comparison to bourbon.
Nose A delicate nose offers buttered toast, spices and some fruits. Clean and refreshing lemon zest.
Taste Fruit and nut. Medium-bodied; sweet but not cloying.
Finish Crisp and spicy. Hints of nuts.

Verdict

19

Producer Morrison Bowmore Distillers
Distillery Bowmore, Islay
Visitor Centre Yes
Availability Specialists
Price ■■■

Bowmore

Tempest

Islay's oldest distillery (founded in 1779, or possibly even earlier) retains a floor malting which produces around one third of the malted barley required by the operation. You can take a tour which includes the malting floor and you may be permitted to look into the kiln with its haircloth floor (the perforated metal sheet onto which the grain is spread to be dried). Even with no fire underneath, the whole place retains the richly aromatic, almost pungent, smell of peat smoke.

And that, of course, is what Islay is really all about and what makes the whiskies so special. For my money, Bowmore is one of the better balanced drams produced here and the peat content (measured in parts per million of phenols) is a little lower than some of its more assertive neighbours. Not that this should make you make the mistake of thinking any less of it. This is very fine whisky and is highly sought after – rare and old expressions of Bowmore are one of the most valuable of whisky collectables and feature regularly in whisky auctions. Indeed, an 1850 bottling sold in September 2007 for a then world-record price of £29,400, though not without attracting some controversy and speculation as to its authenticity. Presumably the buyer was happy.

However, you can pick up a bottle of their Tempest – a tasty, cask-strength, non-chill filtered, 10-year-old Bowmore for around £50; something of a bargain. It'll never be worth £29,000 but that's not the point. This is one to drink and savour, and is probably my current favourite from an extensive and impressive range that has enjoyed deserved success in recent years.

Try, if you can, to get to the distillery. The tour is well managed and the bar at the visitor centre offers a stunning view over Loch Indaal, which is capable of soothing the soul of even the most stressed-out urban sophisticate. Incidentally, Tempest is know as Dorus Mor in the USA.

Colour Bright gold.

Nose Peat smoke and salt, hints of orange crème brûlée and honey.

Taste The signature subtle Bowmore peat smoke to the fore, with salt and a playful citrus note.

Finish A maritime farewell, peat smoke over a stormy sea, but clean and fresh.

Verdict

20

Producer	Bruichladdich Distillery Company
Distillery	Bruichladdich, Islay
Visitor Centre	Yes
Availability	Specialists
Price	▪▪▪▪

www.bruichladdich.com

Bruichladdich

Octomore

This is the kind of thing that Bruichladdich do very well indeed. It's also the kind of thing that, until recently, no one else could or would do though the new generation of small-scale craft distillers have taken up the challenge with some enthusiasm.

The idea is very simple. As Bruichladdich themselves explain, it's an attempt to produce 'the world's most heavily peated single malt'. So that's about it really. If you like heavily peated whiskies you've got to try this, and if you don't it's probably best avoided.

I'm reminded of those chappies on the web who consume ever-fiercer chilies with absurdly high Scoville-scale ratings. The equivalent here is the 'ppm' rating – a measure of the extent of the peating level, which refers to the 'parts per million' of phenols in the malt. Now, lightly peated malt would have a ppm rating of less than five; medium would be 5–15 ppm and heavily peated generally means 15–50 ppm.

With Octomore, which is released in batches of up to 12,000 bottles at a time, the phenol levels have ranged up to 258 ppm (release 06.3 Islay Barley). That, as you may imagine, is a lot and whilst the peating level is only part of the story as the cut taken from the still plays a large part, it certainly comes through into the glass. Just to add to the fun they're bottled at cask strength.

The name celebrates a short-lived Islay distillery close to Bruichladdich which, according to the distillery team, would have produced a heavily peated, non-aged spirit. No one knows, of course, but it's a great story. The releases began long before the current controversy over age statements on whisky, and the early releases usually carried an age declaration. More recently, that's been dropped but Bruichladdich seem to have escaped the wider criticism as consumers have looked to the peating level as the fact of interest and largely ignored age.

Right now look out for release 07.4, which comes in at a relatively modest 167 ppm. Specialists may carry a wider selection of the full range but, as quantities were limited and Bruichladdich has a strong enthusiast following, prices can run up to £250 and more.

With so many variants there are no tasting notes here, but you may rely on it being very smoky. Think of this as the Carolina Reaper of whiskies and you won't be surprised – or disappointed.

Verdict

21

Producer	Bruichladdich Distillery Company
Distillery	Bruichladdich, Islay
Visitor Centre	Yes
Availability	Specialists and some supermarkets
Price	■■□

www.bruichladdich.com

Bruichladdich

The Classic Laddie

It's really quite hard to keep up with Bruichladdich, try as one might. It's been a bit of a soap opera and not without drama and probably some tears.

If you're a whisky fan, you'll know that the distillery was brought back from the dead by an independently minded group of very determined entrepreneurs and some passionate Ileachs, backed by deep-pocketed and patient private investors. They took a very single-minded approach, defying most of the rest of the industry's conventional view of the world, they set off on an intransigent, irreverent ride, styling themselves 'progressive Hebridean distillers'.

There followed a bewildering series of releases until, in July 2012, a decade of resolutely independent ownership came to an end when the company was sold to Remy Cointreau. Things have calmed down a little since then but Bruichladdich are still giving us good things – not least their rightly popular gin, The Botanist.

I would have liked to point you towards the 10-year-old version of The Laddie which was to have been their flagship reference product. Unfortunately, it was so good and their cash flow so tight that they under-estimated demand and it has run out.

It's been replaced by this non-aged version. Not, as some would have it, as part of a cynical plot by distillers to deny us aged whisky but because, just to repeat, the 10 Years Old proved too popular. But this is a more than acceptable substitute, so enjoy.

Incidentally, having visited the distillery recently, I want to acknowledge that the new owners have been exemplary in their behaviour – I expect Bruichladdich will go from strength to strength as part of a larger organisation. Most of the original team remain in place and I'd suggest that Bruichladdich has matured rather than compromised its principles. Indeed, they're leading the charge for greater transparency, so all power to their elbow.

Colour Light and bright.
Nose Very floral; wild mint; loads of fruit and a hint of an ocean breeze.
Taste Creamy fruit fudge with a salty edge.
Finish Nicely balanced and consistent, it keeps on giving as the flavours fade slowly away.

Verdict

22

Producer
The Sazerac Company

Distillery
Buffalo Trace, Franklin County, Kentucky

Visitor Centre
Yes

Availability
Specialists

Price
☐

www.buffalotrace.com see also **www.bourbonwhiskey.com**

Buffalo Trace

An outstanding and highly-awarded distiller of Kentucky Straight Bourbon, the Buffalo Trace distillery was founded in 1857, though there was distilling on the site some seventy years earlier. Buffalo Trace has the distinction of being the first producer of single-barrel bourbon with the 1984 release of Blanton's.

A number of brands are produced here as well as Buffalo Trace and Blanton's: Eagle Rare, Rock Hill Farms, Hancock's, Elmer T. Lee, Sazerac Rye and W. L. Weller, among others. But it is the distillery's own label that we're concerned with, first introduced in 1999. It found rapid acceptance and acclaim. Today they can boast on their website that the distillery 'is the most award-winning... in the world, garnering more than 300 awards for its wide range of premium whiskies'. Impressed? I know I am.

At the heart of it is this fine example of Kentucky Straight Bourbon. The distillers believe that certain floors of some of their warehouses produce the best spirit (romantically, they are named as warehouses C, I and K), and small batches of the best casks are selected for Buffalo Trace. These go through a further selection by a taste panel and as few as 25 barrels are then married and bottled.

Interestingly, the three warehouses share similar construction: they are rick warehouses constructed from large wood beams and surrounded by a brick shell. Each has an earth floor (like a dunnage warehouse in Scotland) and, during the winter, steam is pumped throughout the warehouses to compensate for the dramatic drop in temperature. This has the effect of forcing the whiskey to mature faster – which is just great because it gets to us that little bit quicker!

Buffalo Trace is well distributed in good specialists in the UK. I'd say it was the perfect introduction to bourbon, after which other brands at this price point will disappoint.

Colour Light bronze. No added colour.
Nose Vanilla, mint, spice and some citrus hints.
Taste Sweet with vanilla, cinnamon, brown sugar and oak wood.
Finish Quite long and drying.

Verdict

23

Producer	Burn Stewart Distillers Ltd
Distillery	Bunnahabhain, Islay
Visitor Centre	Yes – modest facilities at the distillery
Availability	Specialists
Price	▢▢▢

www.bunnahabhain.com

Bunnahabhain
18 Years Old

I am inordinately fond of Bunnahabhain. I once spent a wonderful holiday there in one of the former distillery cottages (sadly, they aren't available to rent any longer) and it is one of the quietest and most relaxing places that you'll ever find.

The distillery itself is more functional than picturesque, but it lies at the heart of a pretty bay, with exceptional views over the Sound of Jura. Since I spent time there, Bunnahabhain has been sold by Highland Distillers to Burn Stewart, a small Scotch whisky distilling company ultimately owned by South Africa's Distell (after some 'exciting' years in the hands of a Trinidadian concern who found themselves in something of an ongoing pecuniary embarrassment situation). This has been a thoroughly good thing.

Previously, it was rather dwarfed by its glamorous stablemates, The Macallan and Highland Park. Now it may be in a smaller pond, but it's a bigger fish and all the more comfortable for that. The established distilling team largely stayed intact (though the late, and sadly missed, John McLellan moved on to turbo-charge Kilchoman) but an injection of TLC followed the transfer of ownership and some interesting whiskies were quickly prised out of the warehouses.

Where once there was only a somewhat anodyne 12-year-old version, today there are several aged expressions and occasional – and usually interesting and rewarding – special editions. Recommended here for its blend of quality and value is the 18-year-old style. This is not heavily peated, though the distillery is experimenting with this style. If you like peat, look out for what they call their Mòine or Toiteach styles (hard to find, though).

If you ever get to Islay, it's easy to forget about Bunnahabhain, which lies somewhat out of the way. That would be a mistake: it's well worth a visit, though the road can present challenges.

Colour Bright, rich gold.
Nose Hints of honey and nuts; soft, elegant, with mild aromas of sherry.
Taste Caramel toffee, old leather and oak. A salt influence may be detected, with mint and sweet spice.
Finish Well-balanced, drying, with sherry and spice notes. Slight hints of fading smoke.

Verdict

24

Producer	Casa Cuervo
Distillery	The Old Bushmills Distillery, Co. Antrim
Visitor Centre	Yes
Availability	Specialists
Price	■■■■

www.bushmills.com

Bushmills

16 Years Old

Does it actually matter when a distillery was founded? I mean,
if you thought that Bushmills dated from, say, 1784 rather than, say,
1608 would you buy any less? The distillery makes great play of the
earlier date, emphasising it on their bottles and labels, while being
rather coy about the fact that this relates to a generic licence to distil
in their general area and that the Bushmills trademark doesn't first
appear until 176 years later. Well, what's a century or two among
friends? After all, their competitors have all disappeared and 1784
was a very long time ago. To be fair, the website does clear up the
1608 thing, so we'll let them off.

Bushmills, now part of the Cuervo stable after previous owners
Diageo 'swapped' it for control of Don Julio tequila, is Northern
Ireland's last surviving distillery – and a large and successful one it is
at that. Having survived a huge fire, Prohibition, a vigorous
temperance movement and competition from Scotch whisky,
Bushmills has entered its fifth (or possibly third, depending on the
above) century in great shape, so ownership by a Mexican group
shouldn't present any real problems. From what I hear, the Bushmills
folk are largely in control of both brand and distillery anyway.

The standard Bushmills and the slightly premium Black Bush are
both blends (curiously, the grain whisky comes from the Republic
where it's made at Midleton, by their great competitor) but the
distillery offers three 100 per cent malted barley single malts, at
10, 16 and 21 years of age.

There is an excellent visitor centre at the distillery and, by
taking the tour, you can see triple distillation in action. From
the Bushmills range, I've selected the 16 Years Old single malt.
The extra age and up to a year's finishing in port wood add colour
and depth of flavour to what is already very fine spirit. The 21
Years Old is much harder to find and significantly more expensive.

Colour The attractive ruby red tint is a clear signal of
port finishing.

Nose Waves of fruit on the nose, immediately appealing
sweet notes and some wood gets through.

Taste More fruit, but also malty caramel toffee and
some chocolate. Medium to full-bodied.

Finish Sinuous waves of complexity – a reminder of all
the flavours in the glass – fading delightfully slowly.

Verdict

25

Producer	Diageo
Distillery	Caol Ila, Islay
Visitor Centre	Yes
Availability	Specialists
Price	◻◻

CAOL ILA™

AGED **12** YEARS

ISLAY SINGLE MALT WHISKY

*Out of sight. In a remote cove near Port Askaig lies Caol Ila, hidden sym away.
Islay's distilleries since 1846. Not easy to find, Caol Ila's secret malt
is nonetheless highly prized among devotees of the Islay style.*

Caol Ila Distillery, Port Askaig, Isle of Islay.

www.malts.com

Caol Ila

12 Years Old

It's great to be able to recommend whiskies like this – virtually unknown little secrets that, once tasted, are never forgotten. Caol Ila (pronounced 'cowl eela' – Gaelic speakers look away, please) must be one of the most dramatically located of all of Scotland's distilleries. It's at the end of a precipitous road just outside Port Askaig on Islay, right on the sea, opposite the island of Jura. From the Manager's office window you can see seals, otters and all kinds of interesting sea birds, not to mention the amazing topography of Jura and the famous Paps (stop sniggering, they're great big hills).

But that's not what makes it so great. This is probably the unsung hero of Islay's renowned whiskies, largely because virtually all of the annual production is required for blending and the owners, Diageo, hardly promote the single malt. They do, however, grudgingly release some expressions – but these are generally quite pricey if you don't know you like them and are often restricted in availability anyway.

So why not start with the standard 12 Years Old? It's probably the best balanced of the Caol Ila expressions and a classic of its kind. In common with most Islay single malts it's for lovers of smoky whisky. Like its better-known neighbours at Lagavulin, Laphroaig and Ardbeg, it's a forceful, peat-soaked monster, but some drinkers find it a little sweeter than these.

There are some other versions, including an unpeated version (why bother?), but this is the one you're looking for. If you like this you can move on to its big brother at 18 Years Old and then try one of the many merchant bottlings that are out there. But this is the place to start.

Colour A light-coloured whisky.

Nose The sweet malt hits one initially, followed by peat, treacle toffee and gentle lemon/citrus.

Taste Medicinal, but not aggressively so; wet grass, linseed oil and smoky wood. Add water to release sweet biscuits and more smoky, meaty notes.

Finish Peat smoke and lemon pudding battle it out to the end!

Verdict

26

Producer	Chivas Brothers Ltd
Distillery	n/a – this is a blend
Visitor Centre	No
Availability	Specialists and duty free
Price	■■■■■

www.chivas.com

Chivas Regal
25 Years Old

You get what you pay for, or so the saying goes. Here you pay rather a lot – typically around £180 in the UK, to be precise – around four to five times the price of its junior partner, the 18-year-old style. So what do you get? Apart from a very nice bottle, an extra heavyweight stopper and nice packaging, that is?

Using mainly Speyside single malts, with Strathisla at its heart, Chivas Regal 25 is the creation of Chivas Master Blender Colin Scott who describes it as 'the very pinnacle of the blend'. According to the company, the blend includes a proportion of vatted malts, which have been marrying in wood for what is described as 'a very long period of time'. Scott, widely respected in the industry, has been doing this for a very long period of time himself and has excelled himself here with the pick of the enviable Chivas malt warehouses.

A long-standing favourite luxury blend at 12 years old, Chivas Regal was initially launched by the original owners as a 25-year-old back in 1909 and was arguably the world's first super-premium whisky. Until this release, however, it had only recently been available at 12 and 18 years old. The 25 Years Old is smooth, sumptuous and very rich, with fruit and nut notes, hints of rich chocolate orange and a subtly smoky finish.

With a worldwide release of what is necessarily a limited quantity of whisky, initial stocks were targeted at markets such as the USA and the Far East but you can find this in good specialists. With its handsome presentation, it makes a wonderful and generous gift – if you can bear to part with it!

Colour A rich, dark golden tone.
Nose Orange and ripe peach; Christmas cake and nuts.
Taste Rich and very full, the age showing clearly but with great vitality. Everything from the nose but more. And more besides.
Finish Hints of smoke linger on in a well-balanced and well-mannered conclusion.

Verdict

27

Producer	Diageo
Distillery	Clynelish, Brora, Sutherland
Visitor Centre	Yes
Availability	Specialists and duty free
Price	▫▫

www.malts.com

Clynelish

14 Years Old

Two distinguished judges of whisky established Clynelish's reputation as a single whisky more than 80 years ago: both Professor George Saintsbury (in *Notes on a Cellar-Book*) and his student Aeneas MacDonald (*Whisky*) drew attention to its exceptional quality. Except, of course, that it was not the Clynelish that we drink now that they enjoyed, for the original distillery was actually closed in 1983. To sample anything resembling the spirit that they praise so highly you'll need to find several hundred pounds for a bottle of 30-year-old Brora.

When the owners decided to close the original 1819 distillery, they transferred the name to the new plant. But the old distillery was then reopened in 1967, mainly to produce heavily peated malt for blending, and both produced Clynelish until the Brora name was given to the original distillery in 1975. It was never intended that either should be sold as a single malt but the growing demand for single malts and the distillery's historic reputation persuaded the owners (by then Diageo) to release some limited expressions, which have been enthusiastically received.

Confused? If in doubt, check the price tag – you're looking for the more readily available and affordable Clynelish at 14 years old, which should cost around £40 a bottle. If it's got a three-figure price tag, put it back – carefully.

This is what Diageo refer to as a 'Hidden Malt'. Not that they don't want you to find it at all, it just feels sometimes as if they're determined to make it difficult for you. Actually, they probably can't spare that much because it's a key component in the Johnnie Walker blends. Try the real thing though: charming Highland malt with a maritime note from its seaside location.

Colour A bright mid-gold.

Nose Spicy and perfumed, with the signature 'candle wax' note loved by fans.

Taste At most medium-bodied, but with a creamy/waxy mouth-coating impact. Floral, exotic fruit and spices, hints of smoke and honey.

Finish A salty, drying, slightly bitter finish.

Verdict

28

Producer	Compass Box Delicious Whisky Ltd.
Distillery	n/a – this is a blend
Visitor Centre	No
Availability	Specialists
Price	▨▨

www.compassboxwhisky.com

Compass Box

Great King Street Artist's Blend

When, in their wisdom, Glenmorangie decided to withdraw Bailie Nicol Jarvie there was a gap in the market for a well-made blend with plenty of toothsome single malts, smooth yet not bland, at an affordable price that you could drink straight or use in cocktails.

Step forward Great King Street Artist's Blend from the folks at Compass Box. Now, I feel they are inclined on occasion to take themselves a tad seriously and they're stretching a point to call themselves 'whiskymakers' (they're blenders if you ask me) but everything is now forgiven. It's one thing to make super scrumptious, lip-smackingly good whiskies in small batches at high prices, which they do very well, but altogether something else to offer up a tasty yet affordable blend that you can serve to the whisky geek in your life with absolute confidence. In fact, I'd be absolutely confident that you could serve it to someone who 'doesn't like whisky' and they'd come away a convert. It really is that good. If they don't like this they're probably a lost cause.

What's more, Compass Box are on the side of the angels. They are campaigning robustly for 'transparency', arguing that drinkers have the right to know exactly what they're drinking, with producers permitted to show a full listing of the ages of every component whisky that has gone into a given product. Currently EU regulations prevent this. People have been asking for this since 1930 at least (Aeneas MacDonald of blessed memory in his wonderful book *Whisky* started the movement) but perhaps the time has come. If you agree, go to their website and register support: every additional name helps.

So what's in this? Well, I'm not going to tell you because if you go to the website you will find the blend explained in great detail. Honestly, if you could get the whiskies you could probably make it yourself. But sit back, pour a generous measure and save yourself the trouble. This is superstar stuff and a great introduction to the Compass Box philosophy.

Colour Pale bronze.

Nose Generous portions of apple crumble and vanilla custard.

Taste Creamy, sweet but not cloying, spice, sweet oranges and bread pudding.

Finish Rich, consistent and rewarding.

Verdict

29

Producer
Distillery
Visitor Centre
Availability
Price

John Dewar & Sons
Craigellachie, Craigellachie, Moray
No
Specialists

www.craigellachie.com

Craigellachie
23 Years Old

This is another of Dewars' 'Last Great Malts' collection, a belated attempt (they acquired the distillery in March 1998) to catch up with the single malt market. In fairness, when they finally did launch this range it was pretty impressive, with three aged expressions coming from Craigellachie alone.

The distillery looms over the road to Dufftown, just above the famous Craigellachie hotel, and for years featured a giant White Horse logo on the exterior. That, by the way, is as close as you will get, as apart from occasional openings during the Speyside Festival there are no public visitor facilities.

The White Horse sign reminded us that this was a distillery built for and on blending. It was designed by the great Charles Doig and opened in 1891 for the remarkable Peter Mackie – 'Restless Peter' as he was known, later remembered as 'One-third genius, one-third megalomaniac and one-third eccentric.' He was, shall we say, both forceful and unconventional – but visionary as well. Craigellachie is in many ways his memorial.

Though I've gone a little crazy here – the others in the range are considerably cheaper – I believe Mackie would approve of this expression. He'd like the tastefully retro packaging; he'd respect the fact that, despite modernisation (of which he'd approve, being interested in progress and innovation), the distillery has retained its worm-tub condensers.

They lend a deliciously oily quality to the spirit, and 23 years of maturation have not tamed the meaty weight of this whisky. It's unapologetically, unashamedly old-fashioned, turning its face away from fashion to the point where abashed fashion returns to cower at its feet. We've waited a long time for the blenders to release their iron grip – and my goodness, we now understand why they were so reluctant to release this – but the wait was worth it!

So pay attention: this is rare, special and of incomparable quality.

Colour Rich and deep.
Nose Ripe pineapple – traditionally a mark of great Speyside whisky.
Taste Sweet and fruity with oily sulphur balance.
Finish Herbal, meaty, very satisfying.

Verdict

30

Producer	Diageo
Distillery	Gimli, Manitoba, Canada
Visitor Centre	Yes
Availability	Specialists and duty free
Price	▢▢

www.crownroyal.com

Crown Royal

There are only two Canadian whiskies in this book; not because they aren't interesting but because, in general, they are hard to find in the UK and – let's be honest – we rather tend to look down on them. This, as we shall see, is our mistake.

Crown Royal is the number one Canadian whisky in the world, and the eighth largest spirits brand in the US – a position it hasn't reached entirely accidentally. It is also found in France, Japan and Korea where the somewhat lurid purple packaging of the velvet bag that it comes in and the regal associations are strongly associated with quality.

Not that the royal link is entirely a marketing creation. This dates to 1939 when the original blend was created to mark a visit to Canada by King George VI and Queen Elizabeth (later known to bookmakers the length and breadth of the land as the Queen Mother). This was in the days when Seagram owned the brand. Today it is in the hands of Diageo and has been produced since 1968 at the giant Gimli distillery, on the edge of Lake Winnipeg, built as something of a high watermark for the ultimately doomed Seagram Company. It's actually worth reading their history as a great example of mistimed decisions and corporate over-enthusiasm.

There are several expressions in the Crown Royal range including a Reserve, Cask No. 16 and the ultra-premium XR (you might just find these in duty-free shops in North America). The standard expression has an enthusiastic following and it's a great ambassador for Canada. What's more, it's often found in the UK in 1 litre bottles, which offer great value.

It must be admitted that the bag is a bit of a problem, especially if you like to display your bottles. Don't let it put you off. Someone on eBay might want it. Somewhere a doll's house needs some vibrant new curtains.

Colour Mid-gold.
Nose Sweet initial impact; honey, spices and red berries. Oak and vanilla.
Taste Medium to full-bodied, fruity with spice hints. Sweet and creamy.
Finish Vaguely pleasant and sweet, drifts slowly to a conclusion.

Verdict

31

Producer	The Edrington Group
Distillery	n/a – this is a blend
Visitor Centre	No
Availability	Mainly USA, Spain and Greece – but fighting back in the UK
Price	☐

www.cutty-sark.com

Cutty Sark
Original

For a while this was the best-selling blended whisky in the USA, perhaps on the back of its availability during Prohibition. Anecdotally, this was largely due to the efforts of noted bootlegger Captain William McCoy whose strenuous efforts to run only the best quality supplies ashore to his thirsty customers gave rise to the phrase 'the real McCoy'. Curiously, it was known originally as 'Scots' whisky.

But, unlike its rather vibrant yellow label, it has faded somewhat in recent years, which is a shame. Its extremely pale colour is out of fashion but there is still plenty to enjoy about this pleasant, light-bodied blend. For one thing, though for years it's been marketed by smart London wine merchants Berry Bros & Rudd, the whisky is actually blended by Highland Distillers and contains a healthy measure of great malts such as Glenrothes, The Macallan and Highland Park.

In fact, Highland Park was actually bought by the blenders back in 1937 to ensure supplies for Cutty Sark, though it has gone on to great success in its own right (see separate entries). In early 2010, Highland's parent, The Edrington Group, bought the brand from Berry Bros who had just relaunched it in the UK, so fans of this light and refreshing whisky can have high hopes for its future.

Until now, the main effort has been on the standard product, recommended here, but there is also a range of older styles available. You'll find Cutty mainly in London's smarter style bars and cocktail establishments and this is a hint about how to enjoy this whisky. Undemanding yet of excellent quality, Cutty Sark is the perfect pre-dinner dram and it also mixes well. Don't be fooled by the pale colour – there's more here than meets the eye.

Incidentally, Bill McCoy probably post-dates 'the real McCoy' but it's a nice story.

Colour A very pale golden whisky, set off by the elegant, tall, clear glass bottle and striking yellow label.

Nose Vanilla and some cereal notes.

Taste Delicate and very subtle – a great aperitif whisky.

Finish Crisp and clean.

Verdict

32

Producer	Whyte & Mackay
Distillery	Dalmore, Alness, Ross-shire
Visitor Centre	Yes
Availability	Specialists
Price	■■■■

www.thedalmore.com

Dalmore

King Alexander III

Though we haven't heard so much about this recently, Dalmore used to make great play of their claim to be the most expensive malt whisky in the world. The one-off 'Drew Sinclair' bottling sold for £125,000 and two of the 'Trinitas' expression fetched £100,000 each. Mind you, at the time of writing, a well-known retailer will exchange exactly that amount of your hard-earned for the third and final bottle and Harrods are offering 12 bottles of Dalmore in a bespoke cabinet for a cool £987,500. Hold me back…

So we've established that they have quite a few high-priced and ritzy expressions. High priced whisky ain't necessarily great whisky though, but if buyers will confuse price with quality the whisky industry will keep producing these 'luxury' offerings. After all, the only reason that we now have whiskies at £10,000 a bottle is that there are people who want to pay that. But these are trophies, not whiskies as most of us understand the term.

It's nice to dream though and once in a while crack open a pricey bottle. But I think I can save you around £9,850 because with this King Alexander III you are getting something really quite special and, though it pains me to say it, undervalued – at least by today's standards. While it doesn't carry an age statement you'll have to look past that and consider the remarkable dexterity of the blending.

Dalmore's Richard Paterson has worked overtime on this, combining six different cask types to create the final vatting. That's a one-off. I can't think of anything else so complex or byzantine in its creation. It's slightly mad, but magnificent, to even consider working with spirit matured in ex-bourbon casks, Matusalem oloroso sherry butts, Madeira barrels, Marsala casks, port pipes and Cabernet Sauvignon wine barriques. Going on to actually carry it off is a superb achievement of virtuoso blending that either requires a lot of skill or amazing luck. Trust me, it's the former.

You won't want to drink this every day. It calls for, and deserves, a special occasion – but simply opening it makes the occasion special.

Colour Rich, dark, enigmatic.
Nose Even richer, darker and more alluring.
Taste Thick-cut orange marmalade, vanilla, crème brûlée, vine fruits… it keeps giving.
Finish Majestic oak and spice.

Verdict

33

Producer	Diageo
Distillery	Dalwhinnie, Dalwhinnie, Inverness-shire
Visitor Centre	Yes
Availability	Widespread international availability
Price	▢▢

www.malts.com

Dalwhinnie
15 Years Old

Dalwhinnie distillery lies just off the main A9, the arterial route from Edinburgh to Inverness and its shiny pagodas are clearly visible from the road. But try not to look, because this is one of the more dangerous sections of a dangerous road. Instead, turn off a mile or so to the south and spend an hour touring the distillery and looking at the small displays.

The owners, Diageo, lay much stress on the fact that the distillery is one of the highest in Scotland, though the precise significance of this escapes me. It is not as if lower atmospheric pressure will influence the whisky but it seems to have some romantic value in marketing. In fact, the reason for the remote location is rather more prosaic: the original distillery, then known as Strathspey, was put here to take advantage of the railway, a hugely significant influence on Victorian distillery construction, even if the spinmeisters would rather talk about water!

The distillers themselves claim that, 'Dalwhinnie is situated between the gentle, grassy style of the Lowlands and the austere, firm body of Speyside, which begins some 25 miles to the north. The style is that of the Highlands; a resilient marriage of gentleness and spirit.' That perhaps undersells the merits of this silky, mouth-coating spirit.

Interestingly, the distillery used to employ copper worm tubs to condense the new make. They were replaced in 1986 but the impact on spirit character was such that the change was reversed in 1995. So, twenty-one years on, it's a moot point as to the effect on the current bottling but, such is the demand for the single malt expression in Diageo's Classic Malt Collection, supplies will probably have reverted to worm-tub condensed spirit by the time you read this.

Colour Yellow gold.

Nose Immediately appealing; gentle smoke with honey, ripe fruits and grassy heather.

Taste Often said to appeal to those who 'don't like whisky', this is actually more complex than it first appears and offers hidden depths of vanilla with subtle orange suggestions.

Finish Some smoke surprises, then gives way to a sweeter finish. Perhaps dark chocolate also.

Verdict

34

Producer
Distillery
Visitor Centre
Availability
Price

Burn Stewart Distillers Ltd
Deanston, Doune, Perthshire
No – tours by appointment
Specialists

www.deanstonmalt.com

Deanston

12 Years Old

It's not often recalled that Perthshire was once a major distilling centre, with over 100 distilleries recorded. Today there are still six in operation – Deanston is the one everyone but the most hardcore enthusiast will forget.

It makes it onto this list as one of the most improved whiskies I can call to mind, coming from a distillery as interesting as it is obscure. But ignore any references to 1785. This is when the original building was erected, but it was a cotton mill, designed by Richard Arkwright and powered by the fast-flowing River Teith. Today Arkwright's cellars, which are listed, provide ideal conditions for the maturation of whisky and the distillery is still powered by turbines driven by the Teith. In fact, the distillery generates more power than it needs – enough electricity to run 400 houses is sold to the National Grid.

The mill was converted to a fully working distillery in 1966 and the first spirit ran in 1969 from two pairs of large bulbous pot stills, capable of distilling three million litres of alcohol a year. The large boiling balls on the stills encourage a high degree of reflux, leading to a light and fruity spirit character. The original intention was to use this in launching a major new blend, but this never happened.

Deanston was first released as single malt in 1974 and, by stages, was developed to a 12-year-old product. But, to be blunt, it wasn't terribly good. Not bad, but neither interesting nor memorable.

With the newly released version, however, things are looking up. The strength has been increased to 46.3% abv, it's not chill filtered any longer, it's married in new oak for some weeks prior to bottling and there's no added colour. It's a lot better and worth a try. Still quite light and delicate, but then you don't want some roaring peat-soaked monster or huge sherry character every day.

Colour Yellow gold.

Nose Fresh and fruity, with malt, hints of honey and nuts. Fragrant and quite floral.

Taste An ideal aperitif. Gingerbread, spices and liquorice.

Finish Long, quite dry and pleasantly herbal, with new wood notes at the back.

Verdict

35

Producer
Distillery
Visitor Centre

Availability

Price

John Dewar & Sons Ltd
n/a – this is a blend
Dewar's World of Whisky,
Aberfeldy, Perthshire
Good in the USA, specialists
and duty free in the UK
■■■■■

www.dewars.com

Dewar's
Signature

I have not recommended many expensive whiskies here, believing that there is plenty to explore below £100 and that, once you get well into three figures, a disproportionate amount of the cost goes into lavish packaging (on which everyone in the distribution chain takes a margin, not to mention VAT). Moreover, you can pay a significant premium simply for rarity or age, without necessarily seeing a commensurate improvement in the whisky.

Signature (it's the original John Dewar's, by the way, though I fancy his flamboyant son Tommy would have liked the style of this) does have rather a lavish wooden box and fancy stopper, and it will typically cost you around £250 in the UK (try and find it at the airport instead). But, for those special occasions and if you like this style of whisky, it's worth it.

Like Johnnie Walker Blue Label (its closest competitor) this is non-aged: that is to say that while the blend has some very old whiskies, mainly Aberfeldy, it also has some younger ones and the blenders think you probably wouldn't pay the price if they put the age on the bottle. And even if they don't think that, the marketing people certainly do.

The original blender of this, Tom Aitken, laid great stress on the 'marrying' process whereby the component whiskies spend some months vatted together to allow the flavours to harmonise and this, together with a high percentage of single malt, especially the honeyed Aberfeldy, accounts for the smooth rich taste. It's one to sip and savour after a celebration dinner.

Keep the posh wooden box, by the way; it makes a handy coffin for a pet hamster or gerbil.

Colour Deep golden amber.
Nose Sweet, balanced, rich and fruity, fudge, coffee crème brûlée and vanilla ice cream drizzled with warm toffee sauce. The aromas develop with nougat, toasted macadamia nut, marzipan and lashings of honey.
Taste Rich, sweet and long with a velvety, creamy mouth feel. Butter toffee and honey with warm winter fruits and mellow tones of sultanas, raisins, apples and coconut. Full-bodied and velvety.
Finish A long and complex finish. Smooth and warming.

Verdict

36

Producer	The Sazerac Company
Distillery	Buffalo Trace, Franklin County, Kentucky
Visitor Centre	Yes
Availability	Specialists
Price	

www.buffalotrace.com see also **www.bourbonwhiskey.com**

Eagle Rare
17 Years Old

American whiskey brands can be confusing to the outsider: first seen in 1975, Eagle Rare was originally a 101-proof 10-year-old Kentucky straight bourbon whiskey (not single-barrel) from Seagram and thus among the last new bourbon brands introduced prior to the current era of so-called 'small batch' releases. Subsequently, Eagle Rare has been distilled, bottled and/or marketed by a number of companies, including the Old Prentice Distillery of Frankfort, Kentucky.

The Sazerac Company, a New Orleans-based producer and importer and the parent company of five distilleries, acquired Eagle Rare from Seagram in March 1989. At that time, Sazerac's Kentucky distillery was known as the George T. Stagg Distillery but today carries the name Buffalo Trace (see separate entry).

There are two versions: a 10 Years Old and this older, more expensive big brother, part of Buffalo Trace's Antique Collection. It will come as no surprise to whisky enthusiasts that this book keeps referring back to Buffalo Trace as the source for some outstanding whiskies, but it is perhaps not as well known (yet) to the general consumer as it should be, and the plethora of brand names and identities don't help.

Be that as it may, 17-year-old bourbon is a rare and precious thing. Most bourbon matures much faster than this, due to the Kentucky climate, so age alone attracts a fairly stiff premium, though, in fairness to the distiller, it must be remembered that evaporation losses are higher here than in Scotland. At 17 years this is probably reaching its peak and, for sheer smoothness, has few equals.

Inevitably there is variation from batch to batch, as this is produced in small quantities, but the overall standard is exceptionally high and lovers of great, full-flavoured bourbon looking for well-balanced maturity are unlikely to feel disappointed.

Colour Deep, rich, copper gold.
Nose Honey, caramel and marzipan.
Taste Lots of weight and body; sweetness then orange and vanilla fudge.
Finish Extended finish, surprisingly drying to the end.

Verdict

37

Producer   Heaven Hill
Distillery   Bernheim, Louisville, Kentucky
Visitor Centre   Yes
Availability   Specialists
Price   ▪▪▪

www.heavenhill.com see also **www.bardstownwhiskeysociety.com**

Elijah Craig
Small Batch

Originally 12 years old and 94 proof, but now a NAS, Elijah Craig is bottled exclusively from a dumping of barrels, all drawn from the middle to upper floors of Heaven Hill's traditional metal-clad rick houses. The distillery proudly claims that this is the original small-batch bourbon, having been created before the term was invented. Not so long ago Elijah Craig was awarded Double Gold at the San Francisco World Spirits Competition and has been a winner in *Whisky Magazine*'s Best of the Best tasting competition.

There's an interesting story behind the name. The Reverend Elijah Craig was born in Orange County, Virginia, sometime around 1740 (accounts vary, as if you cared). He was ordained a Baptist preacher in 1771 and must have been a lively character because he was apparently imprisoned briefly in South Carolina after being charged with disturbing the peace during his sermons!

Later he led a congregation to Scott County, Kentucky, and planned the settlement that would eventually be known as Georgetown. Quite the proto-typical social entrepreneur, old Elijah founded a number of businesses including a small distillery that converted bulky grain into whiskey – higher value and easier to transport and trade. Among his ventures was the Royal Spring Mill and, so the story goes, a fire there led to barrels being charred. Rather than discard them, the parsimonious cleric employed them to age his whiskey. (Quite why the barrels burnt from the inside is a mystery: we'll attribute it to divine intervention.)

Anyway, in honour of his contribution to whiskey, Craig is considered a 'Father of Bourbon' and Heaven Hill named this premium expression after him. That's all. It's a pretty fair memorial, however, since it's rightly very highly rated and a great-value bottle.

Colour A rich, warming golden brown.
Nose Lots going on here, with caramel and honey to the fore. Sweet but not cloyingly so.
Taste Agreeably complex, lots of oak notes, spiced fruits and jam. Very smooth and mouth-coating.
Finish Vanilla sweetness; lingering pleasantly and holding together well. Yummy!

Verdict

38

Producer
Distillery
Visitor Centre

Availability
Price

Highland Distillers
n/a – this is a blend
The Famous Grouse Experience
at Glenturret, near Crieff.
Widespread

www.thefamousgrouse.com

The Famous Grouse

Smoky Black

There seems precious little point in telling anyone about The Famous Grouse, as it has long been established as the UK's bestselling blended Scotch, supported by those vaguely annoying but actually mildly amusing TV commercials with the earworm of a tune – so I won't. If desperate, you can learn more at their website or even visit The Famous Grouse Experience at Glenturret distillery near Crieff, essentially a giant visitor centre, shop, statue of a cat and several restaurants with a tiny distillery somewhere in the middle of it all. They get a lot of coach parties who take selfies with the cat statue.

But something has been stirring in the nest in recent years and the grouse has brought forth a clutch of interesting new fledglings with some discreet test marketing going on as the good people in sales try to stretch the brand (some business jargon for you there). While Snow Grouse, a harshly chill-filtered blended grain, seems to have melted away the Black Grouse is still on the wing (sorry, that's the last terrible pun). Except that in 2015 they changed the name to The Famous Grouse Smoky Black (no idea why, but now I've had to rewrite this entry…).

They've popped a 'rare version of Glenturret' into the blend apparently, but this is mainly an Islay-influenced, peaty dram. Ironic, then, you may think, that Highland Distillers sold their only Islay distillery (Bunnahabhain) in 2003, not that it was at that time particularly noted for peated whiskies anyway.

However, observing the current fashion for smoky whiskies the blenders have fashioned this smooth and aromatic drop, which seems to be finding favour amongst peat freaks not least for its competitive pricing. I'm far from certain how many fledglings there are in The Famous Grouse covey right now, though it doesn't matter: more will have hatched by the time this gets into print (sorry, didn't even try to resist these 'cheep' gags).

Colour A mature, rich coppery gold.

Nose Smoky and spicy but not assertive or harsh.

Taste Pleasantly well-balanced, smooth and mouth-coating, this has some signature Grouse sweetness but develops its own spice and fruit character as Speyside and Islay merge faultlessly together.

Finish Cocoa and spices but with the telltale fading smoke character that is promised all along.

Verdict

39

Producer
Distillery

Visitor Centre
Availability
Price

Glenora Distillery
Glenora Inn & Distillery,
Glenville, Cape Breton,
Nova Scotia, Canada
Yes
Specialists
◻◻◻

www.glenoradistillery.com

Glen Breton
Rare

Oops! Our very first 'glen' and it's not from Scotland.

But, be honest, do you think a bottle reading 'Canada's Only Single Malt Whisky' and bearing a large red maple leaf on the front, together with the words 'Canadian/Canadien' could be mistaken for Scotch? Would you pick up a bottle, get it home and then think 'Doh'? The Scotch Whisky Association (SWA) certainly thought so and fought a long and expensive court battle to have the word 'glen' removed from this product, thus protecting you from the consequences of your own foolishness.

A little harsh, you may feel, since this comes from Glenville in Nova Scotia and the distillery's president is one Lauchie MacLean – there's little doubt who settled this part of Canada, and it wasn't the French. And Glenora can only make 250,000 litres of spirit annually and, for their Glen Breton, they use copper pot stills and barley, yeast and water to make their single malt whisky which is notably different from most Canadian whisky.

Eventually the case was lost, though it did go all the way to the Canadian Supreme Court and the SWA seemed to me less than magnanimous in defeat. Anyway, now you can buy Canadian Single Malt Whisky in Scotland. Few off-licences reported queues of excited would-be Mounties and lumberjacks, however, and the Scotch whisky industry seems to have survived this less than convulsive shock.

According to Glenora spokesman Bob Scott, the company will now 'demonstrate the special ability of the Gaelic Scots of Cape Breton to craft an exceptional single malt whisky, which is uniquely Canadian'. Cue 'The Lumberjack Song'.

We await this David-and-Goliath-type struggle with interest.

Colour Golden amber.
Nose Butterscotch, heather, honey and ground ginger.
Taste Creamy with a good flow of toasty wood, almond and caramel.
Finish Rounded, lingering, faintly sweet, the merest whisper of peat.

Verdict

40

Producer	Campari Group
Distillery	Glen Grant, Rothes, Moray
Visitor Centre	Yes
Availability	Widespread
Price	■■■

www.glengrant.com

Glen Grant

12 Years Old

Glen Grant – no, not a Scottish singer but a long-established Speyside distillery that played a large part in getting single malt established as more than a curiosity. But, strangely enough, mostly in Italy. No wonder then that the Milan-based Campari Group invested €130 million in May 2013 to buy the brand and distillery from Chivas Brothers.

It remains one of the world's top-selling single malts but not one that has featured greatly in the UK market. That's changing, and this 12 Years Old is leading the charge.

By rights the distillery should be better known. It occupies a highly visible position at one end of Rothes' main street; it has a super visitor centre and some interesting Victorian gardens and a great backstory, dating from 1840.

The distillery itself is characterised by the innovative tall slender stills and revolutionary purifiers that James 'The Major' Grant, son of founder James Grant, invented over a century ago. They are perhaps the distillery's greatest strength, generating the light and floral character of the spirit that the Italian market in particular really appreciates. But they're also a weakness, as other global markets have tended to look for something more robust and smoky. Really, it's our loss though if we ignore Glen Grant or write it off as too delicate and effete.

I should also mention the distillery stalwart Dennis Malcolm, the multi-award winning Glen Grant Master Distiller, who was born in the grounds of the distillery in 1946. He has worked there for over five decades, watching owners come and go, while managing operations with an uncommon passion and unrivalled knowledge of the industry. This has been rightly honoured with the award of an OBE in June 2016.

There is a partner 18 Years Old in the new range, and also a 48% abv non-chill filtered 12 Years Old for duty-free outlets. So you have to fly to get the really good stuff but don't forget this entry-level expression and, when drinking, please raise a glass to Mr Malcolm and thank him for his efforts, consistency and quiet style.

Colour Typically pale gold/yellow.
Nose Orchard fruits with citrus hints and nuts.
Taste Refined and delicate but with complexity and balance. Fruit cup dusted with cinnamon.
Finish Apples, nuts and spice.

Verdict

41

Producer	J & G Grant
Distillery	Glenfarclas, Ballindalloch, Banffshire
Visitor Centre	Yes
Availability	Specialists
Price	▢▢▢▢

www.glenfarclas.co.uk

Glenfarclas

21 Years Old

Scottish readers may now relax – this third 'glen' is frae Bonnie
Scotland, as in the glens of home. No relation to the Grants
of Glenfiddich fame but, like their namesakes, the Grants of
Glenfarclas are an example of a dying breed: the independent,
family-owned distiller.

Not that there seems any danger of that changing in the near
future, as the next generation of the family is already in the
business and will presumably inherit the reins in due course.
Current Chairman John L. S. Grant is the fifth member of the
family to own and manage the distillery, and his son George S.
Grant is now Sales Director.

The key point about family ownership is continuity, in distilling style
and in management. With freedom from short-term shareholder
pressure, companies like this (and the Glenfiddich Grants) can
build stocks and take a long-term view of their business.

With Glenfarclas this has paid off with the release of their Family
Casks series – individual cask bottlings representing every year
continuously from 1952 to the present day. Some of the older
whiskies are excellent, and excellent value, even if they breach my
self-imposed £1,000 per bottle mark. But I'm not going to
recommend one of those, tempted though I am to do so. As an
introduction to the Glenfarclas style of sherry-aged Speyside
whisky, try the sublime 21 Years Old. At less than £90 it's a steal
at today's pricing, though I'd personally like to see it offered at a
higher strength than 43% abv.

That's nit-picking, though: if you like full-flavoured, rich but not
aggressive whiskies that just ooze class (and why wouldn't you?)
this one is definitely for you. And, if you love the older-style
sherried Macallans, but not their prices, you simply have to try
this. You may never go back!

Colour Noticeably dark; the sherry casks have been
at work here.

Nose Sherry nose, fruit cake, oranges and sweetness.
Not a hint of over-age or rubber.

Taste Very full and rounded; old leather, dried fruits
and dark marmalade. Layered.

Finish A rich, rolling finish.

Verdict

42

Producer	J & G Grant
Distillery	Glenfarclas, Ballindalloch, Banffshire
Visitor Centre	Yes
Availability	Specialists
Price	◼◼◼

www.glenfarclas.co.uk

Glenfarclas
105

I haven't listed too many cask-strength whiskies because they're often quite hard to find, but this is clearly one to try and represents great value for money too. The appeal of the 'cask-strength' bottle is that you are able to try whisky just as you would if you sneaked into the warehouse and got a dram straight from the barrel. It hasn't been filtered, which inevitably removes some of the natural body from the whisky, and self-evidently it hasn't been diluted.

As this isn't a bottling of a single cask, the distillery takes a number of casks and vats them to hit the 60% abv target. It's probably one of the easiest of the very high-strength whiskies to find and was certainly one of the first to offer this style. It gets marks just for that – and for being matured and bottled at the distillery.

So this is strong stuff. But the point is not to indulge in macho posturing and drink it at this strength (though you've got to try a wee sip); rather, you should dilute it to your taste and still pick up all the oily richness that is whisky's natural condition. And while you're doing that, you'll be helping to support that rarest of beasts: an independent, family-owned, Scottish Scotch whisky company. Hurrah!

Glenfarclas are great advocates of sherry casks and this is a minor classic from a family company justifiably proud of their independence. They jealously, and rightly, guard their reputation for quality and you won't ever see anything second-rate with their label.

The distillery is well worth a morning of your time if you're ever in the area. Actually, I'll go further, as should you – make a special trip, you won't regret it.

Colour Deep gold, revealing maturation in top-quality ex-sherry casks.

Nose Clearly a big whisky, fruity with wine notes, caramel and chocolate.

Taste Sherry wood clearly, but honey in the background; sweet chocolate and dried fruits.

Finish Some smoky hints, lingering wine notes and honey shows through.

Verdict

43

Producer	William Grant & Sons Distillers Ltd
Distillery	Glenfiddich, Dufftown, Banffshire
Visitor Centre	Yes
Availability	Worldwide
Price	▪▪▪

www.glenfiddich.com

Glenfiddich
18 Years Old

This isn't a particularly venerable distillery (it was founded in 1886 and therefore missed out on a review by the indefatigable Alfred Barnard) but it is a very, very important one. Glenfiddich is one of the best-selling single malt whiskies in the world, thanks to a far-sighted decision by this staunchly independent family-owned company to start promoting single malt whisky well before the industry giants. For a long time it was number one but has recently been overtaken by The Glenlivet from industry giant Chivas Brothers. That's by volume, by the way; Glenfiddich still sells more by value. These things matter. It's generally said that serious efforts to sell Glenfiddich started in the 1960s but I have seen a promotional bottle pourer from before World War 2, suggesting that at least some lucky drinkers were converted to the appeal of this splendid dram in an age of ubiquitous blends. The distillery was one of the first to be open to the public, a thoroughly good policy that was rapidly copied by others.

However, Glenfiddich's all-pervading presence actually serves to put off some malt fans, who argue that something so popular can't really be that good. Because Glenfiddich is seen everywhere (and it really is) it loses its snob appeal.

But any whisky anorak taking this approach is missing some rare treats. As a family-owned company, William Grant & Sons have been able to take a long-term approach to the stewardship of their whisky, without the pressure of half-year earnings reports to a greedy and often short-sighted City. The result is that the company have extensive stocks of older Glenfiddichs, which are arguably under-appreciated by some drinkers and thus represent something of a bargain.

If your wallet will stretch, some of the older variants are simply outstanding. But, for affordable everyday drinking that gives real pleasure, look no further than this 18 Years Old. It's Speyside at its best; a great example of a classic whisky from a distiller to whom all whisky fans owe an extended vote of thanks.

Colour Rich, warm gold.
Nose A classic Speyside – fruity, fragrant and with a very clean nose.
Taste Lots to find here: apples, sharp citrus notes but plenty of depth also, with dark fruit and oak.
Finish Elegant and well defined.

Verdict

44

Producer	Ian Macleod Distillers Ltd
Distillery	Glengoyne, Dumgoyne, nr Killearn, Glasgow
Visitor Centre	Yes
Availability	Specialists
Price	■■■■

www.glengoyne.com

Glengoyne
21 Years Old

I have a great fondness for Glengoyne for no better reason than it was the first distillery I ever visited. It was on my honeymoon, as it happened, which should have alarmed my wife, though whisky didn't start to play a big part in my life until some years later. She does mention it from time to time, however.

All this was rather more than 21 years ago, so we presumably got something right. The distillery itself has taken on a new lease of life since it was sold by the Edrington Group to the current owners who have invested heavily in the excellent visitor facilities (there's a splendid Crapper in the Gents toilet), increased production and introduced new products. A private company, Ian Macleod Distillers don't answer to the City and so can take a long-term view: as they like to say, '100 per cent family-owned. 100 per cent Scottish. And 100 per cent free to do things our way.'

Once upon a time, they made great play of two facts about their production: all the malt used was Golden Promise and it was totally unpeated. Now, Golden Promise is a low-yielding barley prone to disease, but traditionally always highly rated for making whisky. However, in 2008, as their production expanded, it was quietly dropped, leaving these older whiskies as the final resting place of this old-fashioned variety.

Nevertheless, regardless of variety, this is a very attractive whisky that deserves to be better known. It's available at various ages but really comes into its own with this 21 Years Old style. If you absolutely need to splash out (as Mrs Buxton suggests I may have to quite soon) there was also a 40 Year Old, in a rather nice decanter. Fortunately that appears to have sold out. Perhaps I could compromise with a £2,600 bottle of 35 Year Old. Or not…

Colour Glorious old gold. The judicious use of 100% sherry oak gives richness and depth.

Nose Sweet and honeyed; sherry, ripe apples and maybe baked apple pie.

Taste Toffee, vanilla and rich sherry notes initially, giving way to some spice and a very pleasant warming glow. 'Stewed pears and custard' have been reported.

Finish Quite extended, smooth and warming, with gentle spice hints as it fades.

Verdict

45

Producer	Ian Macleod Distillers Ltd
Distillery	Glengoyne, Dumgoyne, nr Killearn, Glasgow
Visitor Centre	Yes
Availability	Specialists
Price	◼◼◼

www.glengoyne.com

Glengoyne
Cask Strength

If you've got this far, you'll realise I need something special with which to toast Mrs B. Glengoyne fits the bill, not because it's the 'world's best whisky' (incidentally, there's no such thing – it's a silly idea), but because… well, if you've read this far you'll know why. I'm a sentimental old thing at heart.

So it needs to be something robust, full-flavoured and magnificent in an old-fashioned kind of way. Like Mrs B. in fact. And at first I thought I'd found it in Glengoyne's Teapot Dram. What could be more fitting than three fingers of a 58.7% abv sherry-soaked monster? Surely, any woman would be thrilled to be saluted in such a manner and then, shortly afterwards, observe her inamorato slumped on the sofa, mumbling incoherently. Or possibly not.

But then I realised I'd have to return to the distillery to get it, and pay around £90 for the privilege. After which I noticed that I could get two bottles of their Cask Strength for a few pounds more. Problem solved! All the bang and only half the bucks!

Well, only in part. Glengoyne release their Cask Strength expressions in batches (as do a number of distillers) and this means there can be gaps in availability and slight changes in flavour between releases. In general they work with a mix of sherry casks, non-chill filtered and uncoloured (why would you with good sherry casks?), aiming to deliver up something around 58% abv. That makes this great value and you have to consider the inevitable variations between batches as all part of the fun – the tasting notes below aim to describe the general style.

As we go to print I'm happy to report that I'm still married. To the same person, that is.

Colour Dark gold. As I was just saying, judicious use of 100% sherry oak give richness and depth.

Nose Ripe fruits and vanilla pods. Bold and forceful sherry wood notes to the fore.

Taste Thick and creamy, smoother than the strength would suggest. Dark brown sugars but power above all.

Finish Keep an eye out for those viscimetric whorls (© Charles Maclean).

Verdict

46

Producer	Chivas Brothers Ltd
Distillery	Glenlivet, Ballindalloch, Banffshire
Visitor Centre	Yes
Availability	Different expressions widely available
Price	▢▢▢▢

www.glenlivet.com

The Glenlivet
21 Years Old Archive

Glenlivet make much play in their marketing of the claim
'the single malt that started it all'. Like most marketing claims,
there's some truth in there, but perhaps somewhat embellished.
This statement refers to the assertion that the distillery's founder
George Smith was the first licensed distiller under an important
1823 Act of Parliament. Well, so what exactly? Since then the
distillery has been expanded beyond recognition and production
methods have evolved more than a little.

Smith's Glenlivet was always a by-word for quality, though,
and not for nothing is this particular whisky allowed to style itself
'The' Glenlivet. So I think he'd probably still be proud of the
whisky produced under his name, though what he'd make of its
French ownership it might be kinder not to speculate.

The Glenlivet style is characterised by what is generally identified
as a 'pineapple' note and that has been highly prized by blenders
and drinkers for more than a hundred years. With the older styles,
that fruit note can still be detected but the whisky has greater
richness and subtlety. The impact of extra aging and wood quality
can be seen in deeper flavours of chocolate, fruit cake, dried fruits
and then some engaging and complex spice notes, which, for me,
are a hallmark of older Glenlivets and a real stamp of quality and
drinking satisfaction.

Stocks of this style seem to be running low so you may have to
search a bit to find a bottle – you could, of course, always visit the
distillery which sits in splendid isolation in the eponymous glen.

The Glenlivet has recently overtaken Glenfiddich as the world's
bestselling single malt. However, do not be confused by its
ubiquity, as this is a very great and rightly famous whisky indeed.
Expressions such as this superb 21 Years Old have built its
reputation, and innovations such as the Nàdurra range (see next
entry) allow enthusiasts to explore the variety and range of flavours
that a distillery such as this, on very top form, can exhibit.

Colour Pale copper.
Nose Panacotta, ripe plums, dark orange and Christmas cake.
Taste Prunes, subtle coconut; rich and full-bodied with
fruity tones. Add water slowly.
Finish Long, rolling flavours holding together well for an
extended finish.

Verdict

47

Producer	Chivas Brothers Ltd
Distillery	Glenlivet, Ballindalloch, Banffshire
Visitor Centre	Yes
Availability	Different expressions widely available
Price	◼◼◼

www.glenlivet.com

The Glenlivet

Nàdurra Oloroso

Nàdurra means 'natural' in Gaelic and, as the distillery says, the range is all about an unadulterated whisky experience – it's the nearest thing you can get to taking a time machine back a hundred years or so, landing in a warehouse and sampling straight from the cask.

The pioneers of this style were the Scotch Malt Whisky Society but the first *brand* to offer a single-cask bottling at cask strength was Glenmorangie in 1991 with their groundbreaking, but sadly short-lived, Native Ross-Shire expression. Full disclosure: I worked for Glenmorangie then and this was all my work (apart from the small matter of actually distilling it, of course). Sadly, my colleagues never really got it and after my enforced departure following a difference of opinion with the then-MD it was smartly withdrawn. Ahead of my time, I suppose.

Anyway, The Glenlivet now does this type of thing really well. These are not single-cask releases but very small batches at cask strength, designed to explore and showcase different aspects of flavour through alternative peating or maturation regimes. There's lots to explore as the distillery now offers Nàdurra as First Fill (new American-white-oak casks), Peated Whisky Cask (does what it says on the label) and this oloroso cask bottling. In addition, as there have been a number of batches over the years, you may find other styles, such as the 1991 Triumph (single-barley variety), a 16-year-old expression and so on. There are lots to experiment with until you find your personal favourite. Glenlivet's Alan Winchester has excelled himself with these cask selections – not for nothing does his signature appear on the packaging.

So, though I've picked the rich Nàdurra oloroso version you don't have to agree. It uses first-fill oloroso sherry casks from Jerez and is as good an example of the impact of wood on whisky as you'll find, with no chill filtering or added colour to distort the distinctive Glenlivet flavour.

Colour Dark amber.
Nose Vine fruits, rich fruit cake, dried fruits.
Taste Liquorice, Seville oranges, spice and intense dark chocolate.
Finish A suspicion of the Glenlivet pineapple lingers under the oaky finish.

Verdict

48

Producer	LVMH
Distillery	Glenmorangie, Tain, Ross-shire
Visitor Centre	Yes
Availability	Different expressions widely available
	■■□
Price	

www.glenmorangie.com

Glenmorangie
Quinta Ruban

Glenmorangie strikes me as a company undergoing an extended process of transition following its sale to the French luxury marketing house Louis Vuitton Moët Hennessy (LVMH) in 2004 for £300 million, a price which excited some comment.

Previously, the company had something of a schizophrenic personality: trying to maintain Glenmorangie and, to a lesser extent, Ardbeg, as premium whiskies but also attempting to compete with cheaper blends and fulfilling substantial supermarket business.

However, LVMH are more single-mindedly a luxury brand operation and as a result, they have reduced effort on blends, sold Glen Moray, and reformulated, repackaged and relaunched the Glenmorangie range in an attempt to seduce more international buyers. One casualty of the charges was the highly regarded Bailie Nicol Jarvie blend, which is no more. It is sadly missed.

In recent years there have been many special releases, including some quite experimental expressions created by the baroquely titled Head of Distilling and Whisky Creation, Dr Bill Lumsden. Quite why they can't have a Master Blender like everyone else escapes me, but perhaps the point is that they don't want to be like everyone else – and who can blame them?

These exotic offerings, often with unpronounceable Gaelic names, tend to enjoy a brief flowering before they are replaced with something new. They offer insights into cask treatment or the aging process but unless you're a hard-core Glenmorangie enthusiast they can be confusing.

Of the whiskies, the Quinta Ruban is perhaps the most interesting. Glenmorangie pioneered the now wildly fashionable practice of finishing whiskies in alternative casks with their first Port Wood finish back in 1990. That was good; this is an improvement – if no longer the original, it's still the best.

Colour A rich, warm reddish gold.
Nose Archetypal Glenmorangie delicacy and complexity with a new depth.
Taste Great balance; complexity and richness; fruit notes, chocolate and an underlying, delicate sweetness.
Finish A lingering and enigmatic finish that intrigues.

Verdict

49

Producer

Distillery
Visitor Centre

Availability
Price

Irish Distillers Group for
Mitchell & Son
Midleton, Co. Cork
Retail shop at the CHQ Building,
Dublin
Rare
▢▢

www.mitchellandson.com

Green Spot

Think of the coelacanth, a living fossil that was supposed to have died out millions of years ago yet turned up in a fishing net and astounded scientists. Well, this is the coelacanth of whiskey – a dogged survivor from a virtually extinct race of giants.

For this is Irish pot-still whiskey and, by rights, it shouldn't exist. A pot-still whiskey is one made in Irish copper stills (generally larger than those found in Scotland) using malted and unmalted barley (unlike Scotch, which is purely malted barley). This gives Irish pot-still whiskeys a smooth and oily character, with a purity caused by triple distillation.

Traditionally, Irish retailers sold their own distinctive blend of whiskey from casks purchased from a local distiller. But as the Irish industry was rationalised (i.e. closed down) these idiosyncratic one-offs were snuffed out. Eventually only Mitchell's, a long-established Dublin wine-and-spirit merchant, kept going with their wonderful Green Spot, made for them by Irish Distillers entirely from 7- to 10-year-old Midleton pot-still whiskey, a good part of which was matured in sherry casks. It remained pretty obscure, unloved by all but the truly enlightened. Until recently so little was made that it was simply too much bother to kill it off.

It was in fact the sole survivor of this style of whiskey. But then Irish whiskey started a welcome recovery and some marketing genius finally recognised the jewel that they had ignored for so long. I salute that person, especially if they had read my 2010 review!

Today Green Spot has been joined by expressions from Redbreast and Midleton and by a Yellow Spot (a tasty 12 Years Old). And the news gets better: as supply has been increased the price has been slightly reduced. In fact, it's around 20 per cent cheaper than when I first wrote about it here, and it was a bargain then.

The label has been smartened up as well, so even this is no longer a coelacanth, more a sleek and graceful dolphin.

Colour Pale gold.
Nose Greengage jam; clean.
Taste Quite unique! Waxy, lively and full of honey and minty notes; very clean.
Finish Disappears quite quickly, but the sweetness lingers with, curiously, some smoke.

Verdict

50

Producer	Diageo
Distillery	Cameronbridge, Leven, Fife
Visitor Centre	No
Availability	Widespread
Price	▪▪

Haig Club

Haig Club? Seriously? What am I thinking about? This is most assuredly a marketing exercise, complete with celebrity endorsement, stand-out packaging and glitzy lifestyle promotion aimed at an audience, largely Asian, as an introduction to drinking whisky.

If you joined up various bits of Diageo PR, that was made explicit. The brand has been developed 'in partnership with global sporting icon David Beckham and British entrepreneur Simon Fuller' (i.e. they have skin in the game, earning from long-term sales not just picking up a fee for endorsement) and is designed primarily to break into the lucrative Chinese market. 'With Haig Club we have a brand which we believe can unlock the "with meal" occasion in China and open it up to international spirits,' Diageo CEO Ivan Menezes told Deutsche Bank, continuing, 'the blend was created to match with food and seafood in China… our choice of David was down to the extraordinary name recognition he has in China.'

The product itself is a grain whisky, light in colour and sweet in taste and despite an endorsement – 'Forget everything you thought you knew about Scotch…' – from one whisky expert, Western whisky drinkers greeted its appearance less than enthusiastically. Was that testimonial somewhat ambiguous: new consumers seemed unconvinced by the initial £45 price – bottles were soon being promoted at lower prices. As this book goes to press a budget version, Clubman, is about to be launched, designed we are told for 'up-tempo trendy stand-up occasions'. That actually means with masses of ice and cola.

It's not particularly astute to observe that this is whisky for people who don't really like whisky. Whether a tattooed ex-footballer is the best choice of front man isn't for me to say (though I would like to see him actually *drink* some) but it feels as if the brand is in extra time here and yet to put the ball in the net.

I actually think this is a shame. Not because it's my personal favourite but because I salute any effort to free drinkers from the tyranny of vodka; recognise that not everyone is going to jump straight to Lagavulin, say, and acknowledge some radical thinking might just be what whisky needs to carry it into the future, even though the noise you hear is poor John Haig revolving in his grave.

Try it in a cocktail. As for tasting notes, as taste isn't really the point I think we should move on.

Verdict

51

Producer	Suntory
Distillery	Hakushu, Japan
Visitor Centre	Yes
Availability	Specialists
Price	■■■■■

THE HAKUSHU SINGLE MALT WHISKY AGED 18 YEARS

白州
"はくしゅう"

Distilled and matured at Hakushu distillery surrounded by forest

PRODUCT OF JAPAN
SUNTORY LIMITED
ウイスキー

www.suntory.com

Hakushu

18 Years Old

Suntory's second distillery was built in 1973 in Hakushu, at the foot of Mount Kai Komagatake in the Southern Japanese Alps, surrounded by pine forests and close to fast-flowing mountain streams (*hakushu*, pronounced roughly 'hack shoo', means 'white sand banks' and white is Japan's most sacred colour). Hakushu Higashi (East) was added in 1981 and the single malt produced here is held in high regard, though the original plant was mothballed in 2006. For a brief period, this was said to be the largest single malt distillery in the world.

Twelve pot stills operate at Hakushu East and, in the Japanese manner, their varied design allows the distillery to produce spirit with a remarkably wide variety of flavours. Malt is prepared off-site at Yamazaki, from grain brought from Scotland. There are extensive visitor facilities at Hakushu, with an interpretation centre, gift shop, restaurant and a museum, housed in a dramatic former malting noted for its distinctive and unusual double pagoda roof with linking bridge.

We see both the 12- and 18-year-old expressions in the UK with, very occasionally, sightings of the 25 Years Old and some limited bottlings in specialists. Any of these would be a fine introduction to Japanese whisky, but try to find the 18-year-old version if possible, because the additional maturation has really added some extra dimensions to this fine whisky. That may prove difficult as stocks are limited and demand for Japanese whiskies has soared in recent years. But persevere. It's worth it, even if the price has jumped dramatically since I first recommended this.

It has impressive awards from the International Wine & Spirits Competition (IWSC) and International Spirits Challenge and is very highly rated by commentators. The style is quite delicate, attributed by some to the impact on distillation and maturation of the distillery's height above sea level (700 metres). Being neither a physicist nor a meteorologist, I don't feel competent to comment on the accuracy of this intriguing observation.

Colour Pale gold.
Nose Sharp green apples; delicate and refined.
Taste Deceptively light-bodied but with fruit and cereal in great balance. Peat merges with oak.
Finish Spicy and lingering. Some tasters remark on a resemblance to Irish pot-still make.

Verdict

52

Producer	Highland Distillers
Distillery	Highland Park, Kirkwall, Orkney
Visitor Centre	Yes
Availability	Pretty widely available
Price	■■■■

www.highlandpark.co.uk

Highland Park
18 Years Old

Originally I listed four whiskies by Highland Park in this book. Four. From one distillery? Had I taken leave of my senses? And now that I've dropped two, does it mean I only love them half as much?

Of course not. But while you could make a case that this is the best whisky in the world (if there is such a thing), and the distillery has won more awards than I can be bothered to count, a lot has changed in the last six years and I needed the room for other exciting drams.

But let's not forget that, back then, when I asked my 'oracles', Highland Park was their runaway winner, gathering nearly twice the nominations of any other brand. Quite a few of the people who voted for it are competitors, so that's pretty impressive.

I don't actually buy the 'best whisky in the world' malarky, so I'll content myself with saying it's pretty damn fine. You're going to have to look far and wide to beat this stuff. There are several reasons why. The distillery somewhat pretentiously refer to these as their 'five keystones' so we descend dangerously close to marketing-speak here, but bear with me. They talk about traditional floor malting, aromatic peat, cool maturation, sherry oak casks and careful cask rotation.

Thing is, it's not just marketing froth. I've looked back in history and they were doing most of this stuff as early as 1924 and probably well before that; it's just that they didn't bang on about it. So, with Highland Park you get a very traditional style of whisky from a privately owned Scottish company in a funky, modern bottle that keeps getting better the more time you spend with it (the whisky, not the bottle).

Finally, it's on Orkney, which is a special and unique place: a string of islands linked by causeways, ferries and planes; scattered with ancient monuments and a thriving craft community. And another distillery (see Scapa). What's not to like?

Colour Medium bright gold.
Nose A sweet, 'come hither' nose; sherry and marzipan.
Taste Fruity, rich, sweet and agreeably complex.
Great depth.
Finish Smoky hints fade gently into the background.

Verdict

53

Producer	Highland Distillers
Distillery	Highland Park, Kirkwall, Orkney
Visitor Centre	Yes
Availability	Specialists
Price	◼◼◼◼

www.highlandpark.co.uk

Highland Park

Harald

Hurrah! Here's a slightly more affordable Highland Park, and as it's a NAS expression the distillery aren't directly constrained by stocks of a certain fixed age, allowing them to concentrate on flavour delivery, so hopefully it will stick around.

But who is this Harald, I hear you enquire. Well, this is part of a Highland Park series of releases named after Viking warriors; six in all. If you're a collector you'll also want to find Svein, Einar, Sigurd, Ragnavald and Thorfinn. Except you might want to think twice about the latter two, as they are €400 and €1,000 respectively, and that's a lot of Danegeld.

Despite being a great king with a feared army, Harald was killed at the Battle of Stamford Bridge in September 1066 where his invading Norwegian army were defeated by the English troops of the more famous Harold. But unfortunately the victorious English army didn't do quite so well three weeks later at Hastings and that has rather overshadowed this Harald's place in history. However, it's a lot less embarrassing to ask for one of these in the pub than a 'large Ragnavald'.

There have been quite a number of releases from Highland Park in recent years and the marketing people seemed to be getting carried away with Viking-themed packaging. I had my doubts about a few of these but my spies tell me that things may calm down in the foreseeable future, emphasising the core range.

Harald is commemorated in this dram with a vatting of both American and European wood, being fifty-fifty first fill and refill and almost exactly fifty-fifty European- and American-oak sherry casks. So you find some sweeter notes in there alongside the spice, oak and gentle Highland Park smoke. I'd like to see this at 46% abv or even higher, but it was a winner in the 2015 World Whiskies Awards and represents a more accessible entry point to the brand, still one of my great favourites.

Colour Relatively light, bright gold.
Nose A trifle subdued, but stick with it for Garibaldi biscuits – dried fruit and cereal.
Taste Fresher fruit, hints of smoke and stewed apples.
Finish A memory of Christmas past.

Verdict

54

Producer	William Grant & Sons Distillers Ltd
Distillery	n/a – this is a blend
Visitor Centre	No
Availability	Specialists and duty free
Price	■■■

House of Hazelwood

18 Years Old

Whisky enthusiasts would love to try the whiskies from William Grant's more obscure distilleries, Kininvie in Dufftown and Girvan in Ayrshire, but it's difficult. There are very limited quantities of the Kininvie single malt to be found, but only if you search diligently and are liberal with your credit card, whilst some Girvan single grain has been released under the Patent Still label.

But this delightfully packaged blend, initially restricted to the world of tax-free shopping but due on domestic shelves very soon, may be the most accessible way to try both. The Hazelwood name honours the Dufftown family home of Janet Sheed Roberts (1901–2012), a long-lived scion of the Grant family, founders and owners of these distilleries.

There are three whiskies in the range, bottled as 25, 21 and 18 Years Old expressions and, as Master Blender Brian Kinsman rates this 'perhaps the purest expression of Kininvie and Girvan spirits in the range', it seems the one to choose. Bear in mind that due to its duty-free genesis the bottles are the half-litre (50 cl) size rather than the 70 cl that's normal in domestic markets, but this still isn't bad value for the elegant presentation and the opportunity to sample these rare and unusual whiskies.

The blend was married in Portuguese oak tuns, which has contributed a fittingly cosmopolitan touch to the blend, especially as the distillery claim it was inspired by the luminosity of Paris, allegedly one of the most mesmeric cities at the forefront of the Art Deco movement.

Frankly I have no idea what that means and I'm not sure that I really care. Janet Sheed Roberts sounds like a most wonderful and interesting lady with a charmed life and this is a splendid whisky with which to honour her memory, even if you never met her or visited her charming home.

Colour Delicate gold.

Nose Vibrant vanilla sweetness dominates the nose. Delicate oak adds complexity.

Taste Creamy toffee and vanilla notes enhanced by soft oak undertones.

Finish A long and elegant finish. Approachable, yet refined.

Verdict

Producer
Distillery
Visitor Centre

Availability
Price

Irish Distillers Ltd
Midleton, Midleton, Co. Cork
Two – one at the Midleton Distillery
and also one in Dublin
Specialists
□□□□

www.jamesonwhiskey.com

Jameson

Limited Reserve, 18 Years Old

Jameson is the bestselling brand of Irish whiskey and, under the ownership of Pernod Ricard, has been expanding rapidly. The whiskies comprise a blend of pot-still and grain spirit all produced at the giant Midleton distillery. With a bewildering range of stills, the plant is capable of producing a variety of styles, making the role of the Master Blender particularly significant, especially when a number of different casks then come into play.

Though it's hardly cheap, I just have to let this one through. I had the great privilege of tasting this at its release with the late Barry Crockett who was brought up in a cottage in the distillery's grounds. Until his death he was Irish Distillers' Master Distiller Emeritus and, though officially retired, was called back from time to time to collaborate on rare and super-premium releases. Irish whiskey has lost a great man.

The fact that it immediately picked up a clutch of significant awards proves that this was no flash in the pan. A combination of ex-bourbon and sherry barrels are used, and then aged according to the label for 'at least' 18 years. I can believe it: this is splendidly mature, without in any way exhibiting any signs of being over-woody or tired.

This is of a larger collection of Jameson expressions that has recently been relaunched. Jameson is now marketed as a series of 'ranges', known as the Whiskey Makers Series, the Deconstructed Series (rather worrying that one) and the Heritage Series, which is where this is to be found.

My spies tell me that there may be packaging changes in the wind to bring this old stager into line with the family look of the rest of the Heritage collection, but that the whisky won't change. Let's hope they don't 'reposition' the price.

Colour Deep bronze.

Nose Aromatic Christmas cake, honey, vanilla and toffee.

Taste Cloves, nuts, nutty fudge. A wonderful balance with the bourbon and oloroso sherry casks beautifully integrated into a smooth and harmonious whole. Medium body but complex.

Finish Holds together well as all the flavours linger nicely.

Verdict

56

Producer
Distillery

Visitor Centre
Availability
Price

Diageo
n/a – this is a blend, but 'brand home' is Cardhu
Cardhu Distillery, Speyside
Specialists
◻◻◻◻◼

www.johnniewalker.com

John Walker
Private Collection

One of the nicer things about having more distilleries than anyone else is that you have more whisky. And if you have the bestselling Scotch in the world in a world where everyone is shouting about 'craft' and 'small batch' that gives you an extraordinary opportunity to take some of that whisky and let rip. In a subtle and understated way, of course.

Far be it from me to suggest that the blenders at Johnnie Walker are showing off, but they've dug out some remarkable and rare casks to create a series of special editions that they call the John Walker Private Collection. They only release 8,888 of these beauties. That serendipitous number may have given you a hint where the majority will end up but you can find this, and the earlier releases, in some better UK specialists.

Despite the cost it's worth smashing the piggy bank. These very exclusive small batches are the creation of Walker Master Blender Dr Jim Beveridge, exploring the 'building blocks' that go into the regular Johnnie Walker bottlings. 2014 was smoky, expressing the core character of the blend; in 2015 he highlighted the rare fruit notes of older styles and here he has highlighted an unexpected aspect – the underlying honeyed sweetness of the grain whiskies that give the final blend its elegance and balance.

It's probably my favourite, but at first I was taken aback by the blend's apparent simplicity. It comprises primarily grain whiskies, from Diageo's oldest stocks (four out of the five distilleries have now closed) and just one Highland malt, from casks of great age. But the apparent simplicity was deceptive; this is 'simplified complexity': well over a hundred individual casks, some with scarcely a few gallons remaining, go into the edition.

It's a masterpiece from one of the true gentlemen of whisky apparently at the height of his very considerable powers.

Colour Pink gold (like an expensive watch).
Nose Honey, fruit and a waft of rose garden.
Taste Soft and creamy grain leads, then sweet poached stone fruits.
Finish Toffee apple and sandalwood.

Verdict

57

Producer	Diageo
Distillery	n/a – this is a blend, but 'brand home' is Cardhu
Visitor Centre	Cardhu Distillery, Speyside (it's just along the road from The Macallan)
Availability	Everywhere – if you can't find this you're not trying very hard
Price	▢▢

www.johnniewalker.com

Johnnie Walker
Black Label

In truth, this isn't one of my personal favourites. I find this Johnnie Walker expression and its little brother Red Label a little too intensely smoky for my taste.

But you can't argue with success and this is one of the best-selling premium blends in the world. More to the point, if you ask around the whisky industry Black Label keeps coming up as a favourite or a whisky which other distillers and blenders admire. So, if you like big flavours then this is on your list.

Today Johnnie Walker is part of Diageo who, in 2009, controversially shut the door on close to 200 years of whisky history when they closed their Kilmarnock bottling plant, the traditional Walker home. Cue outrage from the locals and Scottish politicians, but it doesn't appear to have made the slightest bit of difference to the worldwide legion of fans who probably neither know nor care where Kilmarnock is. Sorry, Kilmarnock.

The Black Label blend can be traced back to 1867 when Alexander Walker launched his 'Old Highland Whisky' in a distinctive square bottle and slanting black and gold label. The square bottle proved a great boon to the brand in developing export sales – because of the shape, more bottles could be squeezed into any given space and shipping costs reduced. Of such simple things are legends made.

But there is a lot more to this than just clever packaging. Black Label succeeds not simply as a symbol of affluence and status in many markets but because for many it's the benchmark for a premium blend. This is a traditional whisky that's not to be under-estimated. Personally, I wouldn't take it to my desert island, but a lot of expert judges would.

Colour A medium bright gold.
Nose Maple sweetness with hints of smoke. Malt and citrus.
Taste Robust and forceful, the peaty smoke to the fore but also dried fruits, sherry and vanilla; never unbalanced – power with discretion.
Finish Mellow, spicy and a great late-night dram.

Verdict

58

Producer
Distillery

Visitor Centre
Availability
Price

Diageo
n/a – this is a blend, but 'brand home' is Cardhu
Cardhu Distillery, Speyside
Specialists
■■

www.johnniewalker.com

Johnnie Walker
Green Label

Here's a whisky back from the grave. Rescued by the persistent demands of its loyal consumers and, let's give credit where it's due, the sensible decision by the brand owners Diageo to listen to their plaintive cries.

Following a revamp of the Johnnie Walker range in 2012, Green Label was dropped, except for Taiwan where the 'blended malt' category is a local favourite. Here's a tip: if you hear that your favourite whisky is being 'repositioned' or the range 'rationalised' you'd better snap up a few bottles quickly, because this is virtually never good news for the consumer.

And Green Label, a stalwart of the Johnnie Walker range, had its fans who were duly disappointed to see it removed from the shelves. So kudos to Diageo for bringing it back, and for bringing it back without 'improving' it in any way, shape or form. It's the same Green Label, a 15-year-old blend of Talisker, Linkwood, Cragganmore and Caol Ila, in the familiar square bottle with (as you've probably guessed) a green label. Note that it's that unusual beast, a blended malt (i.e. there isn't a drop of grain whisky in here).

But there's more. Inspired, no doubt, by the success of Johnnie Walker Double Black, a few months later Johnnie Walker Island Green was launched. It's got more of the smoky Caol Ila in the blend, but carries no age statement and, for the moment, is available only in travel retail outlets. But that will change soon enough, mark my words.

So there we have it: if you want the original Green Label then the 15 Years Old is here for you, but if you prefer a touch more peat smoke then the islander is the one to pick. Personally I always liked Green Label and was sorry to see it withdrawn. But there's a good ending to this story and with the addition of Island Green everyone should be happy.

Are you listening, Bailie Nicol Jarvie?

Colour Green. No, not really, more a warm gold.

Nose Rich and warming. Espresso coffee and dark chocolate. Smoky hints.

Taste Bran flakes, ground coffee and toast – breakfast of champions!

Finish Spice, honey and fading woodsmoke.

Verdict

59

Producer	Whyte & Mackay Ltd
Distillery	Jura, Craighouse, Jura
Visitor Centre	Yes
Availability	Specialists
Price	▢▢

www.jurawhisky.com

Jura
Superstition

At the risk of offending the good folks at Whyte & Mackay, I'd say that, in the past, the Jura single malts were nothing to get too excited about. Until quite recently they were pleasant enough, but pretty bland, which, since this distillery was built in the 1960s to create employment and serve the blending industry with a Speyside-style spirit, was no real surprise. Incidentally, you may as well ignore that '1810' date embossed on the bottle as the links to the original distillery are pretty tenuous at best.

However, things have changed. In recent years they have made great efforts to raise their profile and release some more interesting whiskies. The standard 10 Years Old is pretty widely seen but I think we can do better than that. What you want as a starting point is Superstition.

This is a mixture of heavily peated whisky in the Islay style (not originally what Jura was built to produce) and some older casks that add warmth and subtlety. Accordingly, it doesn't carry an age statement, but don't let that or the name put you off. It's pleasantly different from the whiskies on nearby Islay.

Jura itself is notable for being home to less than 200 people and around 5,000 red deer. They wander about everywhere – mainly, it seems to me, on the island's one main road where they can be something of a hazard. Jura was also George Orwell's refuge when he escaped from London to write *1984* and the site of the infamous K Foundation Burn a Million Quid art event. Yes, rock musicians turned artists Bill Drummond and Jimmy Cauty quietly travelled to Jura and burnt £1 million in £50 notes. As you would. Obviously.

I don't think this went down well with the locals, but with their fondness for special editions, Jura really ought to commemorate it: a very smoky dram at £50 a bottle would seem appropriate!

Colour Deep bronze.
Nose Wood smoke, bacon and freshly cut peat. Phenolic notes start to dominate.
Taste Spice, honey, pine and peat flavours mingle with nuts and grassy/floral notes.
Finish Smoke fades in again at the end.

Verdict

60

Producer	King Car Corporation
Distillery	Kavalan, Yuanshan, Taiwan
Visitor Centre	Yes
Availability	Specialists
Price	■■■

www.kavalanwhisky.com

Kavalan
Concertmaster

If you're interested in whisky, you've probably heard of Kavalan, one of the stars of the world whisky scene. They're ambitious and not particularly self-effacing: a giant sign at the distillery's visitor centre claims this to be 'The New Homeland of Whisky'. Bear in mind that around a million visitors annually see that!

Is the hype justified? Well, yes, on the basis of this port-wood-finished little beauty, it certainly is. Not that it wouldn't be improved by taking the strength up a notch, but for an operation that didn't even exist as recently as 2005, it's more than impressive. Actually, if you had started distilling in 1905, you would still be happy to put your name on this.

Kavalan represents a serious investment by its Taiwanese owners and they clearly have big plans. The distillery is ramping up to full production and, by virtue of their far-sighted planning, could double their output at very short notice. Rapid maturation gives them another edge over more traditional producers; it's unlikely that they'll ever be able to offer a 30-year-old whisky, but equally unlikely that they're troubled by that.

Initially, most of their attention was directed towards the Far East and their neighbours in the Republic of China. But they are entering major competitions with great success. And in the last couple of years, with increased volume, they have achieved wider international distribution. You can find around a dozen different Kavalan expressions in top UK specialist retailers.

So, if you want to impress your whisky friends, snap up one of Kavalan's stylish Deco bottles. But when you share it, don't tell them where the whisky came from and see if they're not impressed, and slightly incredulous, when you reveal the truth.

If you're feeling flush, their Solist cask-strength expressions, showing the impact of high-quality cask maturation, are very fine if not exactly cheap. But if this goes the way of Japanese whisky they'll seem quite the bargain.

Colour Warm, reddish gold.
Nose Tropical fruits; light fruit cake and liquorice but with wine hints.
Taste Rich, with a good weight in the body; exceptionally smooth for a young whisky.
Finish Mouth-coating, complex – a great balance of freshness and depth.

Verdict

61

Producer	Kilchoman Distillery Co. Ltd
Distillery	Kilchoman, Islay
Visitor Centre	Yes
Availability	Specialists and online
Price	■■■

www.kilchomandistillery.com

Kilchoman
Sanaig

If we rule out the illicit manufacture of moonshine, this is probably as close as you can get to 'traditional' distilling, at least from the point of view of scale. Kilchoman is the first farmhouse distillery to be built in Scotland for a very long while, and the first distillery to be built on Islay for 124 years. There are now several similar projects proposed on Islay itself, not to mention many more actually operating in a number of different countries, but Kilchoman was something of a pioneer and deserves respect and support for this, if nothing else.

The vision of enthusiast Anthony Wills, Kilchoman began distilling in 2005 and released its first whisky in 2009. All the barley used is grown on the neighbouring farm, which the distillery now owns; there is a floor malting; everything is matured and the finished whisky is bottled on Islay. However, despite recent efforts to increase output, capacity is limited and so supplies are restricted: the Inaugural Release of just 8,300 bottles sold out within days and prices promptly doubled on the secondary market.

However, the initial wave of enthusiasm having passed, bottles of subsequent releases should be more accessible if not widely found, and certainly not any cheaper. Unlike many of their expressions, Sanaig is intended to be continuously and permanently available.

It's named after a small rocky inlet to the north-west of the distillery and complements the Machir Bay release. Where that is mainly matured in ex-bourbon casks here we see the influence of sherry-cask aging, primarily old oloroso hogsheads, which add depth and power to the spirit.

The distillery now has an interesting and growing range of whiskies and, though stocks will be very limited, we may anticipate a 10-year-old release very soon. One bottle has already been auctioned for charity, fetching a total of £10,000 for The Beatson West of Scotland Cancer Centre – distillery manager John MacLellan, who died tragically young of cancer, was treated there.

Colour Light oak.
Nose Plenty of fruit. Some oak wood and smoke in the background.
Taste Quite delicate for Islay. Well-balanced and elegant fruits and peat.
Finish A lovely balance of peat smoke, fruit and sweetness.

Verdict

62

Producer	BeamSuntory
Distillery	Jim Beam, Clermont Distillery, Kentucky
Visitor Centre	Yes
Availability	Specialists and online
Price	

www.knobcreek.com see also www.smallbatch.com

Knob Creek

Knob Creek is another small-batch bourbon, distilled at the large Jim Beam distillery at Clermont, Kentucky. It gets its name, mildly titillating for UK drinkers in a vaguely smutty sort of way, from a creek (stream) about 20 miles from the distillery that ran past Abraham Lincoln's boyhood home. Apparently, Lincoln's father worked in another nearby distillery and Lincoln himself was rescued from drowning in said stream. It seems that no one in the marketing department considered the alternative associations of the name outside of the USA.

Anyway, with that out of the way we can move on to the whiskey. This has achieved a sort of cult status, partly due to the astute management of recent shortages of stock creating additional pent-up demand. You can even buy a t-shirt, itself a limited edition, to commemorate the 'drought'.

Knob Creek was created by the legendary distiller Booker Noe in an attempt to create a pre-Prohibition style of bourbon and also, though the distillers tend to gloss over this bit, to come up with an American offering that would make bourbon fashionable again and compete with single malt Scotch.

In that, small-batch bourbon has been a great success, with this 9-year-old, 50% abv product being one of the category leaders.

Others from Beam Global include Booker's, Basil Hayden's and Baker's. Naturally, their competitors have entered the market with their versions also. As the small-batch handle suggests, supplies of these whiskies can be variable and there may be slight variations in style from batch to batch. It's all part of the charm and they're unlikely to be less than very good.

Colour Mid gold.
Nose Nutty, dark citrus and oak.
Taste Rich, full-bodied and complex. Some spice notes.
Finish A long, consistent finish with a lingering aftertaste.

Verdict

Producer | La Martiniquaise
Distillery | n/a – this is a blend
Visitor Centre | No – Glen Moray has visitor centre
Availability | Some supermarkets
Price | ☐

www.label-5.com

Label 5

Classic Black

In the search for value in whisky it's necessary to look in some unexpected places – the shelves of French supermarkets, for example, where this is a big seller. In fact, whether or not you have heard of it, Label 5 is one of the 10 bestselling Scotch whiskies in the world, clocking up sales of more than 2 million cases annually.

That doesn't necessarily mean it's terribly good, of course, and I'm not arguing that there aren't 'better' whiskies out there. But it is fantastic value and when found on offer for as little as £12 a bottle is impossible to resist. It's produced by the French company La Martiniquaise who launched it as recently as 1969. Again, they may not be a household name but since 1934 the founding family have built the second-largest spirits group in France with sales of more than €900 million and over 1,600 employees, whilst retaining their independent status. It's impressive stuff.

They've invested heavily in Scotland, opening a significant grain-distilling, blending and bottling operation near Bathgate in 2004 and later buying and expanding the Glen Moray single malt distillery. The Label 5 website is clear, straightforward to navigate and includes a simple guide to Scotch whisky and blending. There are also a number of great cocktail recipes, which is where I think this whisky really comes into its own.

Being partial to a good whisky cocktail, I see the argument for using the best whisky you can afford when you want the whisky to shine through; but others require it to be more self-effacing. So, while I wouldn't necessarily use this in a Rusty Nail for example, in something fruitier, more complex or that showcases the flavours of the other components, it hits the spot without breaking the bank. Aficionados may well disagree and I don't expect to find this in the well at the Savoy's American Bar, but for a Friday-night mixologist such as myself, Label 5 takes the risk, cost and some of the mystique out of building a cocktail whilst leaving the fun intact.

Colour Pale yellow.
Nose You don't really seriously nose whiskies like this.
Taste Straightforward, pleasant whisky. Barley sugar; delicate fruit sweetness (Glen Moray?)
Finish Don't worry about it, just finish that cocktail and make another.

Verdict

64

Producer	Diageo
Distillery	Lagavulin, Islay
Visitor Centre	Yes
Availability	Specialists
Price	▪▪▪

www.malts.com

Lagavulin
8 Years Old

2016 marks Lagavulin's 200th anniversary, though those of us with long memories can recall packaging emblazoned with the date 1742. Whatever; let's agree it's old.

And famous. Alfred Barnard praised it and Aeneas MacDonald writes of a man 'who... was kept awake for hours in the night by the prolonged rhapsodies of two Highlanders, men who had nothing else in common in the world but their affection for and praise of Lagavulin'.

It has, he says, 'an almost legendary fame'. That was in 1930 and, if anything, its fame has grown. For fans of the richly phenolic, peaty, salty whiskies of Islay this is *primus inter pares*, though Ardbeg runs it close in the passion of its devotees.

Using barley malted at the nearby Port Ellen maltings Lagavulin is distilled unusually slowly – a process which the makers claim gives 'the characteristic roundness and soft mellow edges'. They certainly take their time over maturation, with the standard bottling being the 16 Years Old. Michael Jackson famously described the taste as 'Lapsang Souchong and fruity sherry'. Sounds good.

However, you might want to get your hands on this limited commemorative bottling. It's an 8 Years Old, apparently because that was the age of a Lagavulin tasted by Alfred Barnard when he swung by in the 1880s; one he described as 'exceptionally fine'. It's virtually the same price as the 16 Years Old however, which has understandably aroused comment on social media.

As to the price of the 8,000 bottles of 25 Years Old just released (£800) the less said the better. Even the distillery's own press release concludes that it's likely to end up 'a beautiful collector's item that will rest comfortably on any whisky connoisseur or collector's cabinet'.

Colour Pale straw.

Nose Maritime and smoke notes, with underlying fresh-cut brown bread.

Taste Light initially, then sweet, warm, tarry wood smoke developing depth and complexity. Lapsang Souchong black tea flavours. Hints of herbal tobacco and fresh mint.

Finish Cedarwood, smoke and sea breezes.

Verdict

65

Producer	BeamSuntory
Distillery	Laphroaig, Islay
Visitor Centre	Yes
Availability	Specialists and online
Price	■■■

www.laphroaig.com

Laphroaig
Quarter Cask

Laphroaig is the first of three distilleries you come to following the coast road round Islay out of Port Ellen, and it presents a splendid sight. There is still a floor maltings on site and excellent visitor facilities (though you really want to eat in the Kiln Cafe at Ardbeg just along the road).

The Quarter Cask bottling is a splendid attempt to re-create a style of whisky that would have been more common a hundred or more years ago when smaller casks were used to mature spirit. This may have been because the firkin cask (holding nine gallons, or around 41 litres) was relatively freely available, due to its use in the brewing industry, or because the smaller cask was more popular for private sales or, as the distillery themselves like to suggest – rather romantically – because they were easier for smugglers to transport! Possibly, all three played their part.

The key point, however, is that whisky matures faster in a smaller cask and the wood has a greater influence (30 per cent more according to the distillers). What is more, in their pursuit of tradition Laphroaig don't chill filter this whisky and they bottle it at a healthy 48% abv. Good on them.

It's a classic Islay malt – salty, peaty, phenolic and very full-flavoured.

The result, in my opinion at least, is a huge improvement on the standard 10 Years Old (40% abv) – it's rounder, more vibrant, fuller and sweeter. Everything you look for in Laphroaig, in fact, and more, proving on this occasion, at least, that the old ways really were best.

Colour Quite pale, like beaten bronze.
Nose Tons of peat smoke, sweetness, coconut cream and some chocolate notes.
Taste Bold and assertive, full-bodied and mouth-coating (higher strength alcohol and non-chill filtering here) but gentle and sweet compared to the 10 Years Old.
Finish Amazingly extended finish, with the peat smoke and some coal fires coming into play. Spice notes and the distillery say 'zesty orange'. Beats me.

Verdict

66

Producer	J&A Mitchell & Co. Ltd
Distillery	Springbank, Campbeltown, Argyll and Bute
Visitor Centre	No – but tours are available
Availability	Specialists and online
Price	◻◻

www.springbankwhisky.com

Longrow
Peated

The original Longrow distillery was an early casualty in Campbeltown's long and sorry decline, but the name at least was restored in 1973 when some heavily peated malt was distilled at Springbank to prove that Islay need not have a monopoly on this style. Eventually the idea caught on and Longrow is now distilled regularly, though not in great volume.

So you could say that Longrow is peated Springbank – except that it isn't. The fact that the malt is peated is clearly the key difference but, unlike Springbank, this undergoes a conventional double distillation. A mix of sherry and bourbon casks are used for maturation to contribute sweetness and spice.

Longrow isn't exactly easy to find, and in the previous edition of the book I recommended their CV style. Well, that has all melted gently away like the mist on a peat bog and now Longrow offer three versions: Red (matured, wouldn't you know, in red wine casks and bottled at 51.8% abv), 18 Years Old and this NAS Peated. It's an evolution of CV so I confidently stand by my previous selection and suggest this is the one to start with.

Like most of the company's 'standard' output it's bottled at 46% abv and non-chill filtered – policies that I can only commend. The result is greater mouthfeel in the whisky and a pleasing oiliness that speaks of the genuine article: would that more distillers would follow this lead. Note to consumers – it's worth the extra cost, which in this case is pretty modest: one of the benefits of low-key marketing, simple packaging and not having to cosy up to the City every quarter.

This is not the most subtle whisky you'll ever encounter but, despite its strength, many tasters find it goes well without adding water. Not as big, bold and assertive as CV but if you've 'done' Islay then this is definitely where you go next.

Colour Mid gold.

Nose Supreme balance between peat smoke, vanilla and cardamom.

Taste Rich and creamy, yet robust, vanilla comes to the fore, then rhubarb crumble, followed by waves of spice and smoke.

Finish Balanced with brine and hints of TCP, with vanilla toffee coming through as the smoke clears.

Verdict

67

Producer	Mackmyra Svensk Whisky AB
Distillery	Mackmyra, near Gävle, Sweden
Visitor Centre	Mackmyra Whisky Village
Availability	Specialists
Price	▣▣▣

www.mackmyra.se

Mackmyra
Svensk EK

Imagine a 'Whisky Village'. Gosh! It would naturally have an amazing-looking distillery; there would be a forest warehouse rather like a hobbit's secret lair, half underground with turf on the roof (hah, Macallan, eat your heart out!); there would be a kiln with peat and exotic wood fires where local barley would be malted; there would be a visitor centre and, naturally, a restaurant serving a vast range of the whisky you've just seen being made, with great local food and food-and-whisky pairing dinners.

That could never be, you say. Well, think again. Such a place of wonder does exist. It's in Gävle in Sweden, about 100 miles north of Stockholm. They also have a monstrous 3-tonne straw goat there. Just thought you should know that.

The distillery at the heart of the Village is Mackmyra, founded in 1999 and today – after some financial strains – once again making its name as one of the most innovative and exciting of the new wave of producers. Being of an experimental turn of mind, they have an extensive range of whiskies, some of which find their way to export markets.

Probably the lead product and the easiest place to start is this Svensk EK, which has evolved from the First Edition which I recommended in the previous edition. This elegant whisky has aged for between six and nine years – the wood regime is complex and includes Swedish oak, new American oak, first-fill bourbon and new oloroso casks.

When first launched, Mackmyra's whiskies tended to be expensive but as production has expanded (and other whisky prices risen) they look increasingly good value, especially when the undoubted quality and the fact that most are bottled at 46% abv are considered. Rightly, this Svensk EK has picked up an enviable hatload of awards.

Their success has undoubtedly inspired other Nordic producers and Sweden now has a very dynamic craft-distilling sector. Mackmyra is on a different scale however as the ambituous and visionary Village project clearly demonstrates.

Colour Watery gold.
Nose Light, fresh fruits and warm croissants.
Taste Meaty spices, with citrus notes and toffee.
Finish Some wood notes emerge as it fades.

Verdict

68

Producer	BeamSuntory
Distillery	Maker's Mark, Loretto, Kentucky
Visitor Centre	Yes
Availability	Some supermarkets and specialists
Price	▢▢

www.makersmark.com

Maker's Mark

This Kentucky bourbon was for some time something of a cult among drinkers on both sides of the Atlantic, driven by the personality of the ebullient Bill Samuels Jr, a direct descendant of the founder. I met him some years ago and it wasn't long before he handed me a gun to look at – an antique as it happened but, for a simple chap like me, it was a somewhat unnerving moment.

It is some years, however, since the distillery was privately owned. Though its marketing likes to give the impression of independence, the company has in fact passed through several corporate hands since 1981 and is today part of BeamSuntory, who also own Jim Beam, Laphroaig and Canadian Club whiskies.

It still appears idiosyncratic, however – styling itself 'whisky' in the Scottish manner; increasing production in 2002 by building a second distillery alongside the first, instead of simply expanding the existing plant; and rotating their barrels within the warehouse levels to achieve more even aging. We'll not mention their ill-fated attempt to cut the strength - a lively response on social media sites put paid to that.

Its appearance is also highly distinctive: a square bottle is capped by red wax, which drips on to the bottle. More importantly, the mash bill recipe does not include any rye, but rather contains exclusively yellow corn, red winter wheat and malted barley. Distillation starts in a column still and is finished in a copper pot still, all of which contribute to the final flavour.

It is particularly appreciated for its comparatively gentle and subtle taste, more mellow than many bourbons. Today it has maintained something of a reputation as a drinker's drink: one for those 'in the know'. Now that includes you.

Colour Amber.
Nose Vanilla and spice, tropical fruits and some sweet oak.
Taste At 45% abv, this is medium to full bodied, with spices (ginger), caramel and mouth-coating oiliness.
Finish Smoke, delicately combining with honeyed fruits.

Verdict

69

Producer
Distillery
Visitor Centre
Availability
Price

Hombo Shuzo Group
n/a – this is a blend
Yes
Specialists
■■■■

www.hombo.co.jp

Mars
Maltage Cosmo

As in recent years Japanese whisky has made a remarkable comeback, comparable almost to the revival of Irish whiskey, it gets more and more complex and harder and harder to understand, at least for the *'baka gaijin'* (that's 'stupid foreigner', in which number I am very definitely to be counted). But I expect it's easier for the locals. Hope so, anyway.

Mars' parent company Hombo Shuzo Co. is a small producer of alcoholic beverages. The Mars distillery was opened in 1985 in the small village of Miyada, around 800 metres above sea level, high up in the Japanese Alps in Nagano, with the aim of producing a whisky with special Japanese characteristics.

However, despite only producing during the winter, whisky distilling stopped after just seven years and did not resume until the wider recovery in the category in 2012. This presents the enthusiast with a choice: try to track down some of the original production, which is in limited supply and naturally now very expensive, or go for something more affordable but very recent.

It didn't take me too long to decide, especially when I learned that this Maltage Cosmo was the hit of the 2015 Tokyo International Bar Show, as the audience there are both discerning and demanding.

This comes on paper as a little bit of a surprise as this is not a pure-bred Japanese whisky, despite the convincingly Japanese-looking packaging. Actually, what we have here is a blended malt, which is also a surprise as Hombo Shuzo have only the one distillery and it would be very unusual for Japanese producers to exchange fillings, as is normal in Scotland.

That's actually where the other malt or malts – we don't know exactly what – come from. So think of this as a true 'world whisky', but with a strong Japanese DNA. It's probably your one and only chance to get even a hint of whisky from Mars.

A deeply sad and embarrassing confession now follows. I haven't been able to obtain a sample to taste in time for my deadline. I did think this was a most interesting-sounding whisky and I was interested in the idea of a Japanese/Scottish blend so I will be trying to track it down and will hopefully report in time for a future edition. Apologies!

Verdict

70

Producer Heaven Hill Distilleries, Inc.
Distillery Bernheim, Louisville, Kentucky
Visitor Centre Yes
Availability Specialists
Price ▢▢

www.heavenhill.com

Mellow Corn

Here's something unusual and uniquely American – the nearest thing you'll get to moonshine that's legal. It's far from the nicest whisky you'll drink, at least compared to the others listed here, but it's cheap, fun and worth trying (if only to understand the beneficial influences of malted barley and aging).

But first, a word of explanation. Before there was bourbon, there was straight corn whiskey. Today, corn whiskey is made with a minimum of 80 per cent of corn in the mash bill and must be matured, if it is matured at all, in un-charred new white oak barrels or refill bourbon barrels. The association is with bootlegging, moonshine and generally depriving the government of their share, so it represents a deeply rooted American tradition, also expressed in popular culture through NASCAR racing and TV shows such as *The Dukes of Hazzard*.

The production of moonshine still thrives, or so one would deduce from the number of home-made stills and associated equipment to be seen on various internet auction sites but, for a long time, the only mainstream legal producer keeping the tradition alive was Heaven Hill – and good on them, I say. Some smaller craft producers have now joined in the fun.

Heaven Hill actually make a range, including Dixie Dew and J W Corn, which seems to be the upmarket one! Georgia Moon comes in the kind of jar your granny used to make jam or preserves and is even cheaper (and rawer) than Mellow Corn; the label on this boasts that it's 'aged less than 30 days', which at least is honest.

Unless you want to save a couple of pounds, Mellow Corn is the one to try. It benefits from two years of aging and comes at a useful 50% abv. Definitely one to serve blind to the whisky snob in your life. Happily, you won't go blind drinking it.

Colour Pale gold.
Nose Waxy (it should be), with lighter floral notes and vanilla.
Taste Surprisingly complex, with mouth-coating oiliness; some fruit and toffee.
Finish Quite lively; the fruit, wood and caramel notes hang on in there.

Verdict

71

Producer	Zuidam Distillers BV
Distillery	Zuidam, Baarle-Nassau, The Netherlands
Visitor Centre	No
Availability	Specialists
Price	■■■

Zuidam
ZUIDAM DISTILLERS

MILLSTONE
DUTCH SINGLE RYE WHISKY

100
RYE
WHISKY

100 Proof
100 Months Old
100 % Rye Grain
100 % Small Batch
100 % Milled by Dutch Windmills
100 % Small Pot Still Distillation
100 % New American Oak
100 % Hand Made

Zuidam Distillers BV
Baarle-Nassau, The Netherlands

700 ML   50% ALC. BY VOL.

Distillation Date: Jan. 2004   Cask type: American
Bottling Date: 22.03.13   Cask number: 600

www.zuidam.eu

Millstone

100 Rye

This small, privately owned, family-run distillery in The Netherlands makes whisky, Genever (naturally), rum, liqueurs and very, very good gin. In fact, everything I've tried of theirs has been very, very good. For something that started very small indeed, in a country with no whisky tradition as recently as 1975, it's a considerable achievement, which other distillers might note.

But the 100 Rye is a standout. The first time I tried it I simply couldn't believe how tasty it was, and I found it hard to accept that it hadn't been distilled in the USA, the traditional home of rye whiskey. I then had the considerable pleasure of introducing it to some Dutch people, and they too were impressed and frankly incredulous that it was distilled by their countrymen.

The label really rams home the '100' message, pointing out that this is 100° proof (i.e. 50% abv), and 100 per cent made with rye grain (49 per cent malted, 51 per cent not), in small copper pot stills, aged in 100 per cent new American oak casks and matured for 100 months (that's just over eight years, to save you working it out). In fact, they might as well have marked it 100/100 on the label and been done with it.

The thing is, as soon as I tried it I would have forgiven them that moment of vanity. The spicy rye is a tricky grain to work with and needs a lot of skill and attention to every stage of the distillation process to get it just right. Zuidam have managed it superbly well. If you like rye whisky, which is a style all on its own, and one you should get to know, then you will love this.

The key flavour is spice: think cinnamon, cloves, vanilla beans – a whole spice market of flavours – overlaid with the fruit and wood.

It has rightly won a number of top awards and I expect it will continue to do so, blazing a path for the new world of craft distillers in unexpected locations. So full marks to Millstone!

Colour Rich red.
Nose Citrus and spice, with fruity hints and honey aromas.
Taste Lots of spice but well balanced and complex.
Oak sings out and complements the sweet fruit.
Finish Pepper and delicate oak.

Verdict

72

Producer	William Grant & Sons Distillers Ltd
Distillery	n/a – this is a blend
Visitor Centre	None – but both Glenfiddich and The Balvenie have tours
Availability	Some supermarkets and specialists
Price	▯▯

www.monkeyshoulder.com

Monkey Shoulder

This isn't really what you'd expect from William Grant, makers of Glenfiddich and The Balvenie. The deliberately funky name (which, as we shall see, has some whisky heritage – but really!), the painfully hip website and the emphasis on cocktails and trendy bars all smack of an achingly self-conscious marketing strategy.

The thing is, it's pretty decent whisky and it appears to have worked so, as the young people apparently say, 'respect'. So what is it? Technically, it's blended malt – that is to say, a mixture of several single malts but no grain whisky (that would make it an ordinary blend). Being in the fortunate position of owning several distilleries, Grants blended some Glenfiddich, some Balvenie and some Kininvie (a third distillery on their Dufftown site they tend to keep quiet about) to create a whisky designed for easy drinking and use in cocktails.

It was created by their Master Blender David Stewart, as traditional a whisky man as you'll find, and is prepared in small batches of carefully selected casks that then undergo further maturation before bottling.

Rather tongue-in-cheekily I feel, Grants refer to it in their promotional literature as 'triple malt Scotch whisky'. They ought to know better, but we'll let that pass. It has been enthusiastically picked up by a number of rather more cutting-edge bars in those markets where it's been released so far and has collected a number of awards.

It's also competitively priced, with fun packaging featuring three monkeys climbing up the neck of the bottle. And the name? It refers to a condition which apparently affected the workers on the malting floor after turning malt by hand. Not, as you might expect, some kind of monkey business.

Find someone who doesn't like whisky and try this on them, perhaps in one of the various cocktails suggested on the brand's website. In fact, go ape!

Colour Bright gold, with copper tints.
Nose Vanilla, lemon zest and fresh fruit.
Taste You'll probably mix it but bananas (no, really), some spice and hints of citrus.
Finish Relaxed and fairly short finish, but holds together well.

Verdict

73

Producer	Diageo
Distillery	Mortlach, Dufftown, Moray
Visitor Centre	No
Availability	Specialists
Price	▣▣▣▣

www.mortlach.com

Mortlach
Rare Old

It's hard to remember just how bullish the Scotch whisky industry was in 2013 and early 2014. Nothing, it seemed, could go wrong. This was a 'golden age' for Scotch with demand riding high and distillery expansion the order of the day. Mortlach was to receive an £18-million investment to double output and, having languished in obscurity for years, a new range of single malts from the distillery – lauded by connoisseurs as 'the Beast' – was to establish Mortlach as '*the* luxury malt to redefine the category' (their words, not mine).

Well, leaving aside what their competitors thought of that, we did get the new whiskies. By October 2014 however the clouds had darkened and though some preparatory work was complete the main construction plans were put on hold.

There are four whiskies in the range and this Rare Old (not that it carries an age declaration) is the entry level, though at the equivalent of around £80 for a standard bottle it could hardly be considered particularly accessible. That's not the point of 'luxury' though; the game involves keeping some people out and, sure enough, the 25 Years Old is priced reassuringly over £800 for a 70 cl equivalent.

At this point you are probably remembering the Flora and Fauna 16-year-old bottling, which not so very long ago was on offer for around £40. No longer: the remaining bottles have been snapped up by collectors and you can add £100 to that.

So is this Rare Old any good, you ask. Well, I reluctantly have to say that yes, it is. It's big, meaty whisky that's true to the Mortlach tradition. The company is evidently playing for big steaks and, while I have a slight beef (puns intended) with the cost of all this, I can't but acknowledge that the spirit itself lives up to the promise of the rather elegant bottle. It will surely impress the oligarch in your life if you offer a glass or two of this full-flavoured Speysider.

Colour Beaten copper.
Nose Nuts, ripe fruits and a sweet Dundee cake.
Taste Plenty of oily mouthfeel with a forceful delivery, packed with dark chocolate and black cherries then pork crackling and barbecue sauce.
Finish Warm and dry, with comforting spices.

Verdict

74

Producer
Distillery

Visitor Centre
Availability
Price

Nikka
Yoichi and Miyagikyo
Distilleries, Japan
Yes at both sites
Specialists

www.nikka.com

Nikka

All Malt

Pay attention: this is very, very interesting and possibly unique. This is a non-aged, blended malt whisky using pot-still malt whisky from Nikka's Yoichi and Miyagikyo distilleries and some whisky distilled in a continuous (Coffey) still at Miyagikyo, from a mash comprising 100 per cent malted barley.

So if such a thing was ever made in Scotland the words 'malt whisky' couldn't appear, as the Scotch Whisky Association (SWA) have determined that malt whisky cannot be made in a column still, even if the still is entirely made of copper and the mash is 100 per cent malted barley. This has led to some controversy with distillers such as Loch Lomond (curiously, not members of the SWA) pointing out the illogicality of this position and some commentators suggesting that this is a bar to both innovation and moves towards a greener, more energy-efficient industry.

I am not alone in arguing that this is horribly reminiscent of the attitude of the British manufacturing industry in the 1950s and 1960s when we still made cars, TVs, ships and so on until hidebound management, intransigent trade unions and complacent politicians allowed imports (often from Japan, as it happens) to take over our markets. This is not to adopt a xenophobic 'little Britain' mentality, but simply to observe that all things change; that innovation is the lifeblood of consumer marketing and that hanging on to some self-serving vision of authenticity, traditional practice and heritage (that owes more to marketing spin than historical facts) may well prove something of a blind alley.

But the cumulative wisdom of the Scotch whisky industry disagrees with me and, as was observed as early as 1930, that comprises a body of men well 'assured of their commercial acumen'. Well, we shall see – I shall be happy to be proved wrong.

Anyway, they are not so hidebound in Japan and so we can try and judge for ourselves. This is something of a bargain and delicious in a gentle, self-effacing sort of a way.

Colour Rich gold.
Nose Clean, delicate with hints of cereal.
Taste Mouth-coating, toffee and vanilla; malty with pear fruit and vanilla development.
Finish Light but consistent and holds together well.

Verdict

75

Producer
Distillery
Visitor Centre
Availability

Price

Diageo
Oban, Argyll and Bute
Yes
Specialists and possibly some
better supermarkets

www.malts.com

Oban

14 Years Old

This is one of the Diageo Classic Malts range, so it hardly needs promoting here. Yet it always seems to me that this whisky lacks the fame and glamour of some of its stablemates. Perhaps the owners don't promote it as heavily, as production is restricted by Oban's limited scale and stocks would rapidly run out if everyone knew just how good this was.

The distillery lies at the heart of this rather charming West Highland town, which has grown up around it, so much so that it's impossible to see how it could now be expanded. But perhaps that's a good thing, as the character can't be changed by growth, and things will go on pretty much as they have in living memory.

There are two 'standard' expressions – a 14 Years Old and the so-called Distiller's Edition, which is finished in sherry casks. There are also occasional special releases such as the Manager's Choice. Frankly, these seem to me rather cynically designed for the collectors' market and there is a growing body of opinion that they might just be a tad over-priced.

But we don't need to worry because it leaves more of the delicious 14-year-old style for us. This is lovely stuff! Bags of complexity, salt and smoke but never unbalanced or over-bearing in delivery; the initial impression is then overtaken by dried fruits and a citric sweetness that fades gently with more smoke and malty notes. Great value at around £40. If you find some of the Islay malts just too much, then you may find this exactly to your taste. Personally, I love it.

If you do go to Oban there's no need to pack spare footwear: the town has more discount shoe outlets than your heart desires. I haven't the faintest idea why.

Colour Mid-gold.

Nose Fresh and clean with a salty tang; some fruit and whiffs of smoke.

Taste Medium body, soft and mouth-coating; initially sweet but develops greater complexity with spice, orange, drifting smoke and dries as it evolves.

Finish Is the salty tang imagined by association? Only another glass can answer this conundrum!

Verdict

76

Producer	Inver House Distillers Ltd
Distillery	Old Pulteney, Wick, Caithness
Visitor Centre	Yes
Availability	Specialists and possibly some better supermarkets
Price	■■■

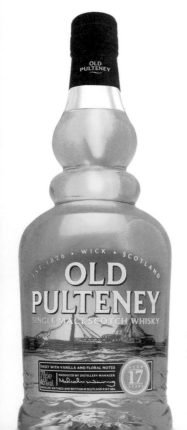

www.oldpulteney.com

Old Pulteney

17 Years Old

'When I got of an age to understand Old Pulteney, I could admire its quality when well matured, recognising in it some of the strong characteristics of the northern temperament.' So observed one of Scotland's finest writers and whisky's most ardent champions, Neil M. Gunn, in his 1935 classic *Whisky & Scotland* (try and read it one day).

Well, Old Pulteney is still possessed of a singular character and nowhere is this seen more remarkably and forcefully than in this 17 Years Old expression. This distillery is located on the coast at Wick and makes much play of its coastal location and the curious flat-topped stills. It has changed hands on a number of occasions during its long life but, today, seems to be really valued by its owners Inver House. They have worked hard to promote the brand and have released a number of interesting expressions, including a venerable 30 Years Old.

But, for its combination of exceptional taste and real value, I'd have to pick their 17 Years Old (there is a 21-year-old version, but it seems to me just a trifle over-aged). To tell the truth, if this teenager was on Islay, whisky fans would be fighting to get it, savouring the piquant, salty taste and the long, lingering finish. Some tasters pick up pineapple and coconut notes, while others praise the sweet/salt balance. Personally, I love the saltiness which then gives way to vanilla and a deliciously creamy, mouth-filling (it's bottled at 46% abv), slightly sweet orange, before fading away gently.

This has won a number of significant awards in the last few years – the judges certainly knew what they were doing. Neil Gunn would love it and he was a fine judge of whisky.

Colour Very pale for the age, but predominantly matured in ex-bourbon wood.

Nose Sweet and yet salty; loads of honey, vanilla and lemon.

Taste Remarkably complex and justifies taking time over it; malted barley notes roll over into some liquorice and chocolate flavours, with a steady drumbeat of salt ever present.

Finish Goes on and on, drying and fading steadily and consistently.

Verdict

77

Producer	Irish Distillers
Distillery	Midleton, Co. Cork
Visitor Centre	Yes
Availability	Specialists and possibly some better supermarkets
Price	■■■

www.irishdistillers.ie

Redbreast

12 Years Old

Let's assume that you couldn't find any Green Spot, though that's a lot easier than it once was – so try again. But if you can't track that down, this is what you need to get – not that this is in any way second best and, at 12 years of age, it has some additional maturity to show off. Again, this is an Irish pot-still whiskey and thus something of a rarity, though you will find Redbreast a little easier to find.

Irish Distillers is today part of the giant Pernod Ricard group and they take their distilling very seriously. You can visit the distillery near Cork, though what you see is actually a museum and visitor centre, albeit a very good one, in the old distillery, which no longer produces. The real work goes on just out of sight at a modern plant with a remarkable range of stills, producing all kinds of spirit (including gin and vodka). Needless to say, you don't get to see that.

Redbreast was originally produced in 1939 for Gilbey's by the original Jameson distillery. But after that closed, stocks of maturing whiskey ran out and the brand was withdrawn. Observing the refusal of Green Spot to die and the upsurge in single malt Scotch, Irish Distillers brought it back as a 12-year-old from Midleton, to general acclaim. A mix of both sherry and bourbon casks go into the blend and the full-on style is a classic of its type.

This is a major award winner and always scores highly in independent tastings. If you're able to splash the cash there is a rich and complex 21-year-old version, bottled at 46% abv, but it commands a hefty three-figure price tag, so I'd suggest that you start here. Or keep looking for Green Spot and save a fiver.

Colour A subtle bronzed gold.

Nose Tons of body on the nose, promising excitement within!

Taste A massive whiskey, but with plenty going on and layers of flavour to explore. Sweet, with lots of ripe fruit and spice notes. Honeyed brioche. Very full and oily for a 40% abv.

Finish Stick with it for waves of vanilla, honey, oak and spice.

Verdict

78

Producer Irish Distillers
Distillery Midleton, Midleton, Co. Cork
Visitor Centre Yes
Availability Exclusive to The Whisky Exchange
Price ▪▫▪▪▪

REDBREAST

SINGLE POT STILL

IRISH WHISKEY

ALL SHERRY
SINGLE CASK

LAID DOWN IN THE *Midleton* DISTILLERY 02/04/1999
BOTTLED *exclusively* FOR THE WHISKY EXCHANGE

Bottle Number 486 of 576

PRODUCT OF IRELAND

www.irishdistillers.ie

Redbreast

All Sherry

Now let's assume I've convinced you about Redbreast (it was the last entry; do pay attention) and let's move on to something unusual. I'm breaking my own rules here because, for the moment, this is available only from The Whisky Exchange (London and online); is strictly limited to 576 bottles and costs £180 (but it is bottled at a mighty 59.9% abv which accounts for some of the cost).

However, I'm including it here because it is so good, and because Irish Distillers have shown themselves so responsive to consumer demand that I have to believe that there will in the future be further releases with greater availability. If I'm wrong and by the time that you read this all the bottles have gone, I apologise. Contact Irish Distillers or The Whisky Exchange and tell them you want more.

Unusually, while the age of the whiskey is precisely known because it came from a single 500-litre oloroso cask, there is no age declaration. It was, however, matured for precisely 16 years, 147 days – so why are the distillery so coy? According to Midleton Distillery's Head Blender Billy Leighton, the decision was taken because the 'number is not particularly relevant. We want people to understand this isn't Redbreast 15, but this is something that can make up the next batch of Redbreast 15.' Got that?

This class of product – a facet of the brand, but not actually the brand – is particularly interesting to whisky enthusiasts because they provide an insight into the mind of the blender and an understanding of how a product is created. To that extent, it's an educational product so think of it as a teaching aid, if that makes the price easier to bear.

However, I did enjoy it in its own right, though it's definitely one to sip and savour and take carefully. As it's waited all that time and bottles are so rare it seems the least one can do! This is a great and classic pot-still whiskey, so let's hope there are some more casks like this in the massive Midleton warehouse complex.

Colour Rich and dark.
Nose Massive. Rum-and-raisin cookies, bitter oranges and burnt caramel.
Taste A real heavyweight but smooth and creamy. Dark toffee, pork kebabs and autumn fruits.
Finish Huge, rolling, balanced.

Verdict

79

Producer	John Dewar & Sons
Distillery	Royal Brackla, near Nairn, Highland
Visitor Centre	No
Availability	Specialists
Price	▢▢▢

Royal Brackla

12 Years Old

Well, it's been a long time coming. Royal Brackla was opened in 1812 and picked up the second of its royal warrants as far back as 1838. In 1930 it was lauded as 'one of the dozen or so best whiskies made in Scotland'. Bacardi, the folks behind Dewar's, acquired the distillery in March 1998 and yet it's taken until now for them to seriously market it as a single malt.

Then they had the gall to present it as one of the 'Last Great Malts'. I suppose it would be if you waited until everyone else in Scotland has got something on the market. However, enough of that.

This is a distillery with a great and noble history, though as it was substantially remodelled in the mid-1960s and then further expanded in 1970, the connection between today's operation and the heavily-garlanded original is somewhat tenuous. But again, enough of that: let's look to the present.

This is the youngest of a range of three recent releases (the others are the 16 Years Old and the 21 Years Old) and very nice it is too. Having sat on their stock for some years, Dewar's can offer a range of ages, which appeals to the cognoscenti, without having to resort to a NAS entry-level expression, and they have chosen well.

According to the distillery they use only Scottish barley. That and the tall stills, lengthy fermentation times and the exclusive use of oloroso sherry casks for maturation do suggest that something quite special is going on here. For most of its recent life the whisky had been used for blending (to be fair, there was a long-term supply agreement with Diageo, the previous owners, that restricted the stock for sale as single malt) and its arrival now, albeit rather late in the day, is something of a revelation.

So make the most of it. Royal Brackla may have taken more than 200 years to come to the single malt party but I suspect it won't be too long before it lives up to the original distillery motto: 'So much famed for its superior quality.'

Colour Pale gold.
Nose Deceptively light. Spicy and warming.
Taste Fruit and nuts, with the Dundee-cake richness of sherry always evident.
Finish Vanilla, black pepper. Great length.

Verdict

80

Producer	Chivas Brothers
Distillery	Scapa, near Kirkwall, Orkney
Visitor Centre	Yes
Availability	Specialists
Price	▢▢

www.scapawhisky.com

SINGLE MALT SCOTCH WHISKY
SKIREN adj. Old Norse, glittering, bright skies

Inspired by nature's bright, **GLITTERING SKIES**,
described in Old Norse as *skiren*, this expression is
exclusively matured in **FIRST-FILL** American oak casks
for a smooth creamy sweetness with a hint of orchard
fruit, citrus and coastal **HEATHER**.

Scapa

Skiren

Dramatically located on Orkney's famous Scapa Flow, the little Scapa distillery has suffered from turbulent history, inconsistent marketing and the dominant shadow of its more famous neighbour Highland Park. It's still worth paying attention to this little gem, however, and to understand some of its history.

In the recent past (i.e. since the mid-1980s) the distillery was owned by Allied Distillers who let it run down disgracefully. It was generally assumed that it would close but, to general surprise, 2004 brought a complete refurbishment. The following year Pernod Ricard's Chivas Brothers acquired the distillery as part of their takeover of Allied. Again, there were rumours of closure or possibly disposal. Hope, though, sprang up amongst lovers of this ugly duckling – perhaps a swan would emerge after all.

For some years, a 14 Years Old expression had been marketed in a desultory and uncaring fashion but it was appreciated by connoisseurs wanting to explore a lighter, unpeated island style that was quite unique. With Chivas' considerably greater marketing expertise and sensitivity to whisky, the brand was relaunched and a 16 Years Old expression released – sadly, not in my view a great triumph though it won some fans.

Because there was insufficient stock to go round all their world markets the decision was taken to bottle at 40% abv. A similar problem arises with the NAS Skiren but let's not be churlish: it's good to see investment in the brand. Rumours are that there will soon be a 'new' 14 Years Old, replacing the current 16 Years Old, to be followed by a 25 Years Old. The definite good news is that the distillery is now open to the public. Hurrah! And don't forget the small display on the long-lost Stromness Distillery in that town's Museum; it's utterly charming.

But if you do visit Scapa, please ignore all the marketing-speak about the Lomond wash still: it really isn't. With its internal plates removed, it's simply a pot still with a rather unusual head and neck. So there!

Colour Warm yellow.
Nose Apples, hints of a sea breeze, buttermints.
Taste Pears, lemon rind, baked apples and a gentle sweetness.
Finish Nutty oak, spices and vanilla.

Verdict

81

Producer	The Spencerfield Spirits Company
Distillery	n/a – this is a blend of various malts produced by Whyte & Mackay
Visitor Centre	No
Availability	Specialists and possibly some better supermarkets
Price	▢▢

THE ORIGINAL OLDBURY

TRADE MARR

SHEEP DIP

BLENDED MALT SCOTCH WHISKY

DISTILLED & BOTTLED
EXCLUSIVELY

SPENCERFIELD SPIRITS CO

40% vol. FOR THE 750 ml

www.spencerfieldspirit.com

Sheep Dip

God loves a trier, or so they say. Well, Spencerfield Spirits are certainly trying.

The company was formed when Alex Nicol, then at Whyte & Mackay but with a long industry career, fell out with his bosses and left. Nothing unusual there but, in place of the usual severance package, he took with him the rights to the unloved Sheep Dip brand, which was then languishing in the corporate cellars, along with a supply agreement for whisky. He's a clever boy: I wish now I'd thought of something similar when my last whisky employer showed me the door! Still, if we're being candid for a moment, writing about whisky is a lot easier than making and selling it and probably suits my personality rather better.

Then he convinced W&M's Master Blender, the ebullient Richard Paterson, to work with him and together they created a new blended malt for Sheep Dip. Back in the day, Sheep Dip had been a cult success, but it relied on independent ownership to give the brand and its customers the necessary time and attention. In corporate hands it just wasn't a priority and it slowly faded away.

Alex and his wife Jane have changed all that. Having got the whisky right, they invested in some dramatic new packaging and an old horse box, which they drive round various country fairs sampling the product and selling bottles. Slowly but surely, it's gathering a new following and once people try a bottle they want more. And so Sheep Dip is slowly and painfully, bottle by bottle, getting back on its feet.

I wouldn't tell you all this if it wasn't also very good whisky. It's a great story and a great whisky from some great people (Alex: will that do?). Oh, and they have a great website, as well, which tells you all this in so much more loving detail.

Colour Rich, warming gold.
Nose Quite floral with honey, malt and fresh fruits.
Taste Dominated by solid Highland and Speyside malts, this has plenty of weight without lacking subtlety or balance.
Finish Lots to look for as the Islay component finally kicks in, adding smoke; some spice lingers also.

Verdict

82

Producer	Diageo
Distillery	Glen Ord, Muir of Ord, Ross-shire
Visitor Centre	Yes
Availability	Distillery only for UK market
Price	▢▢

www.malts.com

The Singleton of Glen Ord

12 Years Old

Here's a singular thing: there isn't just one 'The Singleton' but lots of them. Not just The Singleton of Glen Ord at 12, 15 and 18 years of age, but Singletons of Dufftown and Glendullan as well. To add to the fun we have the funky Tailfire and Sunray.

But, being of a simple turn of mind, we have to choose just one and as it's the most widely distributed of the family and, in these troubled no-age-statement times, has the comforting reassurance of a big, bold age claim, it shall be The Singleton of Glen Ord 12 Years Old. It's complex, light and fruity – easy to drink without being bland or unmemorable.

This comes from the little-known Glen Ord distillery which lies on the edge of the beautiful, but equally obscure, Black Isle, hence the claim that the whisky is made with water from the White Burn and barley from the Black Isle. If you do find yourself in the general area the Black Isle is well worth a day of your time, if only for the unspoilt Georgian townscape at Cromarty and the colony of bottlenose dolphins which can often be observed from the shoreline.

As for the distillery, since its foundation in 1838 it has worked faithfully away, most recently to serve Diageo's many blends. It was briefly part of the Dewar empire and today it is being worked harder than ever; still producing for blends, but increasingly being promoted as an accessible single malt for the Far East.

That does present a bit of a problem though because despite occasional appearances on the shelves of some specialist retailers, this is only generally available at the distillery's visitor centre. So it seems a trip to the Black Isle is in order: architecture, dolphins, interesting historic distillery and great whisky – what's not to like!

Colour Delicate gold.
Nose Red fruits, dried orange peel.
Taste Apples, some sherry richness, black cherries and just a hint of smoke. Moreish.
Finish Sustained fruit notes, chocolate raisins, cinnamon.

Verdict

83

Producer
Distillery
Visitor Centre
Availability
Price

Ian Macleod Distillers Ltd
Unspecified
No
Specialists
▪▪▪▪

www.smokehead.co.uk

Smokehead
Extra Black

Aargh! This is one of those 'Ronseal' whiskies: it does exactly what it says on the chunky tin. I don't really like it but, if your taste runs to big, peaty, smoky monsters then you need to try it. Frankly, I find it all a bit too much, but I can't deny it's a roller-coaster of a dram. Actually, it's more of a weapon of mass destruction – to my taste buds at least. I needed a good night's sleep before the palate was clear and the work of tasting could continue.

For that reason, be warned – this takes no prisoners. It's an 18-year-old Islay single malt (unspecified, but one of the extreme ones) bottled by the excellent Ian Macleod Distillers to take advantage of the current vogue for peaty whisky. I can't imagine what else they'd use this for: the tiniest drop in a blending vat and the taste would dominate the finished product.

There is a little brother, the regular Smokehead. But if you like this kind of thing, why bother with the monkey, when you can have the organ grinder? I saw Extra Black compared to the amplifier that goes all the way up to 11 in *Spinal Tap*. This is just as rock and roll as that. And as pointless, really, unless 11 is where you want to go.

I'll leave it up to you. You have been warned. And it's not particularly cheap either. But that's rock and roll for you.

Colour Curiously pale. I don't think this has ever seen the inside of a sherry cask.
Nose Peat, smoke, more smoke, more peat. Salt. Then peat.
Taste Explosions of spice, pepper and, yes, peat smoke. Just huge waves of peat. And salt.
Finish Excuse me, I have to leave now and get a glass of water.

Verdict

84

Producer	Inver House Distillers Ltd
Distillery	Speyburn, Rothes, Banffshire
Visitor Centre	No
Availability	Specialists
Price	

www.speyburn.com

Speyburn
Solera 25 Years Old

A little-known but traditional and very attractive Speyside distillery, Speyburn deserves wider fame. The 10-year-old style enjoys some success in the USA, as much because of aggressive pricing as anything else, but you hardly see it in the UK, which is a great shame. And our loss.

Another classic Charles Doig design, the distillery was built in 1897, at the end of the great Victorian whisky boom, and for years was part of the DCL. They first mothballed it in response to the over-production of the 1980s (the so-called 'whisky loch'), but thankfully sold it to Airdrie-based Inver House Distillers in 1991.

Most of the spirit goes for blending but the distillery offer this spectacular 25-year-old expression which is, as the saying goes, 'to die for'. It is quite remarkably good. But I owe you an apology. I first listed this in the 2010 edition of this book where I said '...*just snap up a bottle or three and enjoy a rich, luscious, classic Speysider at a tasty 46% abv which, with a better-known name and some sexy designer packaging, would have whisky fans queuing round the block to give three figures for a bottle. In fact, if you poured this into a bottle of -- We'd better not explore that thought any further!*'

At that time you could get a bottle for £70 or so. It was only £80 when I revised the book in 2013.

But, oh dear, the word obviously got back to the distillery because it's now got some snazzy new packaging and comes in a box, with a £250 price tag. I'm sorry – I only hope that you took my advice and put a few bottles by for a rainy day, because now it's pouring.

If it's any consolation I didn't either. Not that you feel any better about it.

Colour Curiously pale for the age, but an attractive light gold.

Nose Soft oak and vanilla. Honey, fruit cake and some light smoke.

Taste Mouth-coating, rich and warm; buttered honey sweetness, burnt orange and delicate oak notes.

Finish Smooth, well-balanced and consistent. Maybe a hint of dark orange, just at the end.

Verdict

85

Producer	J & A Mitchell & Co. Ltd
Distillery	Springbank, Campbeltown, Argyll and Bute
Visitor Centre	Yes
Availability	Specialists
Price	▢▢

www.springbankwhisky.com

Springbank
10 Years Old

Once upon a time the town of Campbeltown was one of the most important and respected distilling centres in Scotland. But, over the years and for a variety of reasons, it declined until only one really active distillery was left – Springbank.

It struggled on during the 1970s and 1980s as something of an anachronism, a historical curiosity, quirky, stubbornly independent and almost wilfully resistant to change. In 1987 the late Michael Jackson recorded that its 'very traditional plant has not produced for some years'.

However, there were always a few die-hard enthusiasts and keepers of the true flame and the owners resolutely soldiered on, oblivious to 'progress'. In those days you could buy your own cask but, sadly, they won't let you do that any more. As the single malt boom gathered pace in the early 1990s, Springbank began to acquire a cult, almost mythic, status greatly enhanced by its remote location and the distillery's hermit-like reluctance to embrace publicity.

The plant is still traditional – in fact, walking round the distillery is like stepping into a Victorian distilling textbook – and Springbank adheres to an unusual 2.5 times distillation process (there is a very good explanation on their website, so I'm not even going to try). This and the floor malting, lack of chill filtration or colouring and labour-intensive production mean that Springbank is arguably the most traditional of Scotch whisky.

In recent years it has flourished and the owners have even been so bold as to open a new distillery, Kilkerran. A range of styles is produced at Springbank and they vary dramatically (see Longrow) but this is the standard and most widely available. A 'must have' whisky if there ever was one.

Colour This has been known to vary according to the casks they use, from pale gold to a darker shade. Don't worry – it's just part of the idiosyncratic fun.

Nose Expect leather, some peat smoke hints, spices and a salty note.

Taste More saltiness, nutmeg and cinnamon, orange peel and, bizarrely, vinegar. But nice.

Finish Slightly perfumed with a sweet/salt tussle going on. Hints of smoke linger at the end.

Verdict

86

Producer	New World Whisky
Distillery	New World Whisky Distillery, Essendon Fields, Melbourne, Australia
Visitor Centre	Yes
Availability	Specialists
Price	▢▢▢

www.starward.com.au

Starward

New World Malt

Here's an Australian whisky so good that Diageo gave them lots of money to make more. Hold on, you say, Diageo already make very good whisky so what's going on?

Well, basically Diageo are very, very large but lots of the innovative stuff and excitement in the whisky market is coming from small producers like Starward. And Diageo want some of that, so they set up an investment arm to seek out interesting small producers and help them grow – with an option to buy them out if they succeed, of course. What did you think this was, altruism?

They spotted something they liked in Melbourne-based Starward, a leading light in Australia's rapidly growing craft spirits sector. They liked the team, the vision, the packaging and they especially liked the product, believing that Starward had the right stuff for global expansion. Hence the cash to help them grow further and faster.

'What they've done,' said the man writing the cheque, 'is to create something which is really distinctively Australian, maturing all their whisky exclusively in Australian wine barrels, and working with Melbourne's "four seasons in a day" climate.'

The barrels are indeed interesting. They're apera casks. Never heard of it? Neither had I, so I looked it up: it's the official new name for Australian fortified wine, once familiar to us all as Australian sherry. But they can't call it 'sherry' any longer if they want to sell in the EU, so it appears it's apera now. Starward's casks are re-coopered, resized and re-toasted before being filled. This, along with that changeable climate, gives plenty of flavours to play with, so expect more variety from these guys before very long.

This is the second Australian whisky in this book. Give them another five years and there will be many more. Whisky is on fire there. Their entrepreneurial distillers have torn up the rule book and are shaking a few trees. What they need is the cash, lots of it, to take on the world. Which is where we, and Diageo, came in.

Colour Rich amber.
Nose What a sweetie! Pears, bananas and apples with juicy raisins and dried figs.
Taste Toasted brioche with red fruit jam. Liquorice root and sandalwood.
Finish After Eight mints, dusted from the spice jar.

Verdict

87

Producer
Distillery
Visitor Centre

Availability
Price

Suntory
n/a – this is a blend
Centres at Suntory's Yamazaki
and Hakushu distilleries
Some supermarkets
■■■

HIBIKI.
SUNTORY WHISKY

JAPANESE HARMONY™
A meticulous blend of the finest select whiskies
43% ALC BY VOL (86 PROOF) 750 mL

whisky.suntory.com

Suntory
Hibiki Harmony

With Japanese whisky suddenly enjoying a remarkable surge in global popularity, demand has outstripped supply. The inevitable result is price rises, the withdrawal in some markets of previously well-established products and their replacement with no-age-statement expressions.

So bid farewell to the Hibikis that previously graced these pages. If you didn't snap one up when the chance was there, well, the chance has gone. However, the good news is that where they were hard to find and relatively expensive, this entry-level style is more widely available and somewhat more affordable, though as ever with Japanese whisky that's a relative term.

What we have here is a blend from Yamazaki and Hakushu with grain whisky from Chita, all beautifully presented in the brand's trademark 24-facet bottle. It's a standout presentation: both very attractive and sufficiently different to draw the eye without being outré or unduly outrageous. I can see it with a candle in the neck gracing student bedsits (if students still have bedsits, that is, and can afford £50 bottles of whisky).

Whisky Advocate magazine in the USA rated it their Japanese Whisky of the Year for 2015. However, that didn't go down well with all of their readers and online responses were harsh: 'boring', 'forgettable' and 'disappointing' were some of the kinder comments.

However, I still think this would probably be a very good first Japanese whisky, but I mention the mild controversy to demonstrate (and this is just one example) how tastes and opinions can vary so radically, and what strong feelings can be aroused on the subject. You really do need to make up your own mind and not be led by the pontifications of the 'experts'. The answer comes as my top tip for really making this book work for you: either buy a mini or taster sample or club together with friends and plan to share bottles and costs. More fun; less money; considerably fewer forgettable disappointments!

I'd still give this a whirl if I were you.

Colour Diluted sunshine!
Nose Lots of crisp fruit. Spice hints.
Taste As promised: fruits and subtle spice.
Finish Restrained and gentle.

Verdict

88

Producer
Distillery
Visitor Centre

Availability
Price

Suntory
n/a – this is a blend
Centres at Suntory's Yamazaki
and Hakushu distilleries
Currently USA only

Suntory

Toki

Do you like a challenge? Then work this out: publicity for Suntory's new blend suggests that it is (and I quote): 'Respectful of heritage, inspired by reinvention, [and] expresses both what is authentic and what is next.'

Whatever does that mean? Here's another challenge: you'll need a trip to the USA to find this because it's currently exclusive to that market. 'Toki' means 'time' in Japanese and that's the clue to the somewhat opaque PR speak above: this is a product designed to promote a revival of the *mizuwari* and highball drinking rituals. If you don't know either, well, essentially they are whisky and water.

Now you may think: whisky and water, what's so special about that? Nothing, I suppose... and yet, done properly and served by a skilled Japanese barman (there are few better) it is a thing of joy, beauty and great simplicity. Look it up on the web and study the videos would be my suggestion as there isn't space here to convey the subtleties and arcane points of the serve.

As to the whisky, Toki is a blend of malts from Hakushu and Yamazaki distilleries with a significant percentage of Chita grain whisky, here working to the fore rather than as a base for the malts. Further complexity is added by the use of several different cask types. So, while the components are superficially the same as found in Suntory's Hibiki, this is a very different whisky created with a different drinking occasion in mind. Clever stuff. Remember, too, that the *mizuwari* is the perfect accompaniment to Japanese food.

Finally, a thought about ice and its special significance to Japan. In times gone by, ice was difficult to store during the summer so was reserved for the Emperor and the shoguns. Today we fortunate commoners can enjoy fantastic chilled serves, none more stylish than with an ice ball – it looks good and the whisky tastes great, provided of course that the correct whisky is selected; the raison d'être of Toki.

NB: Producer's tasting notes (because my sample didn't arrive).

Colour Clear gold.
Nose Basil, green apple, honey.
Taste Grapefruit, green grapes, peppermint, thyme.
Finish Subtly sweet and spicy finish with a hint of vanilla oak, white pepper and ginger.

Verdict

89

Producer	Diageo
Distillery	Talisker, Skye
Visitor Centre	Yes
Availability	Specialists and possibly some better supermarkets
Price	⬜⬜

www.malts.com

Talisker

10 Years Old

Another of the original Classic Malts range from Diageo, Talisker has long been praised for its brazen, up-front, uncompromising flavours. Like a number of the recommendations here, it's a very forceful product indeed.

Personally, they're not my favourites but it's hard to deny that lots of people like them and, once they try this style, absolutely fall in love with it – all the more so, in this case, if you visit the distillery (and you should try to).

Out of the various different releases I'd recommend the 'standard' 10 Years Old as an introduction to Talisker, and then you can move on to the 18 Years Old; the non-aged 'Storm' variant; one of the many limited releases or the excellent Port Ruighe (overleaf).

Talisker has long had its fans: in 1880 Robert Louis Stevenson listed it as one of the three 'king o'drinks', and in his seminal and highly influential book *Whisky* (1930) Aeneas MacDonald had Talisker wrestling with Clynelish for inclusion in his list of the twelve most distinguished of Highland whiskies.

Today the distillery runs along quite traditional lines. It still uses wooden worm tubs and, uniquely, the lyne arms on the wash stills are designed to trap vapours from the first distillation before they reach the outside worm tubs, while a small secondary copper pipe carries the trapped vapours back to the wash stills for a second distillation. Also traditionally, and commendably, Talisker is bottled at higher strength (here 45.8% abv) just to add to the fun.

If this sounds complicated, it's because it is, but all this has a huge, if not fully understood, influence on flavour: the result has to be experienced to be appreciated. Once tasted, never forgotten.

And finally, I see that the price hasn't really increased in the last six years. Well done, Talisker!

Colour Bright gold.

Nose Assertive marine character with waves of smoke.

Taste Surprises with some sweetness, then fruits, smoke and seaweed take over. Some commentators recommend trying it with seafood – oysters or good smoked salmon seem to work.

Finish Lots to give here with the sweetness coming back and a distinctive sharp pepper bite.

Verdict

90

Producer	Diageo
Distillery	Talisker, Skye
Visitor Centre	Yes
Availability	Specialists
Price	■ ■ ■

www.malts.com

Talisker

Port Ruighe

Since the original Glenmorangie effort there have been a number of whiskies finished in port casks. Some are very good indeed (e.g. The Balvenie). But, if they'd asked me if Talisker would work, I would have politely suggested they didn't bother. I would not have expected the robust Skye spirit to form a happy partnership with the more delicate, wine-infused port wood.

However, prepare to be surprised. There are a number of Talisker variants available at present – 57° North, the various Distillers Editions, aged expressions up to a 30 Years Old, Storm (which I rather like) and so on – but for me this represents an excellent balance between a great taste and value. The port cask finishing softens the Talisker fire, rather than (as I would have imagined) being swamped by it, and allows you to explore some fruity notes with the smoke always lingering in the background.

Port Ruighe, in case you were wondering, is the Gaelic for Portree, the principal town and port on the Isle of Skye. Strangely, given the number of distilleries in the Hebrides, Skye doesn't seem to have had much of a distilling tradition and Talisker is the only one operating on the island. That may change soon, however, if the proposed Torabhaig farmhouse distillery originally promoted by Sir Iain Noble comes to fruition. The last reports were that spirit would run in 2017 – we shall see.

But Talisker fans can visit their distillery where it's possible, on occasion, to purchase exclusive bottlings, which makes the journey over the sea to Skye all the more rewarding. However, I can't imagine anything more pleasurable than an evening dram of Port Ruighe, somewhere on a Skye beach with the sun setting in the west. Unless, of course, it was pouring with rain or the midges were out in force – as happens all too often here.

Colour Reddy copper hints.

Nose Ripe stone fruits, chocolate. A suspicion of smoke and a sea breeze.

Taste A medium weight whisky (it's bottled at the Talisker standard of 45.8% abv). An initial impact of fruit and some sweetness gives way to peat and spicy smoke.

Finish The dark chocolate notes linger, dancing a merry jig with smoke and the last of the plummy sweetness.

Verdict

91

Producer Ian Macleod Distillers
Distillery Tamdhu, Knockando, Banffshire
Visitor Centre No
Availability Specialists
Price ▪▪▪

FOUNDED 1897

SPIRIT OF
SPECIAL *Enlightenment* EDITION

TAMDHU

SPEYSIDE SINGLE MALT
SCOTCH WHISKY

BATCH STRENGTH

BATCH Nº: 001

MATURED IN SHERRY CASKS
NATURAL COLOUR

www.tamdhu.com

Tamdhu

Batch Strength

The people who built Tamdhu distillery and the folk who work there today have a 'can-dhu' attitude apparently. At least that's what it says on their website. You can groan now: fond as I am of puns, I wouldn't have imposed that horror on you....

Anyway, described as 'perhaps the best designed and most efficient distillery of its era' Tamdhu was built in 1897 towards the end of the great Victorian whisky boom. Under the original owners, Highland Distillers, it opened and shut again until it was finally mothballed in 2010. That was strange as things were beginning to pick up then, but apparently they wanted to concentrate their efforts on Macallan (just up the road) and Highland Park.

Tamdhu required quite some investment so accordingly it was sold to Ian Macleod Distillers, a small independent Scottish firm who also own Glengoyne, bought some years previously off the same group. Macleod recommissioned and refurbished Tamdhu and reopened in 2013. Previous to that the spirit had been used principally in blending, but with the distillery came some superb sherry casks that needed to see the light of day as single malt. And so Tamdhu Batch Strength was born.

And what a discovery that must have been. So far they've released this as a 10 Years Old which is rather lovely if you like a Speyside whisky of this style (think Macallan or Glenfarclas) but I'd go for this cask-strength edition, which is released in small batches. Bottled at around 60% abv, it simply offers more than the standard: more colour, more mouthfeel; more impact. The packaging is rather striking and the story an interesting and intriguing one of a distillery that one feels is only now coming into its own, after more than a hundred years of obscurity.

So, if you haven't heard of it before, don't worry. It's one to buy with confidence and serve with flair. Go on: you can-dhu it! (Sorry.)

Colour Rich and dark.
Nose Red fruits, nuts, an uncompromising promise of depth.
Taste So much to tell: spicy, but with dried fruits, dark orange marmalade on toast, Crème brûlée.
Finish Rolls majestically on, even if you've added a drop of water.

Verdict

92

Producer   Teeling Whiskey Company
Distillery   Teeling, Dublin
Visitor Centre   Yes
Availability   Specialists
Price   ◼◼◼

www.teelingwhiskey.com

Teeling

Single Malt

There's been no distilling in Dublin since the old Jameson distillery shut down in the mid-1970s (accounts of the closure vary). Those were dark days for Irish whiskey, once the greatest in the world, as sales fell steadily and the industry went into terminal decline.

Or so it seemed. More recently there's been a considerable revival and Irish whiskey is recovering some of its past swagger and dash. But it could never be considered whole until distilling restarted in Dublin, ideally in The Liberties. This was the historic centre of Irish distilling and, in the late nineteenth century, arguably the most important place of its kind in the world.

So it's great to be able to record the arrival of Jack and Stephen Teeling, from the family that rebuilt Cooley, one of the pioneers of the Irish whiskey renaissance. Their new distillery is located on the Newmarket square hence their claim to be the 'Spirit of Dublin'.

Not that we will see any whiskey (they do offer a poitín though) for a few years yet as distilling only started in June 2015. So what is this single malt, you ask.

In short, it's some of the best casks from Cooley that the Teeling family were able to secure at the time they sold that business, bottled under their new name. This rebranding isn't unusual in Irish whiskey and will continue for several more years until more of the start-up operations have properly matured stocks. There's nothing sinister or underhand about it, this is simply the way this market has evolved.

The Single Malt expressions are the Teeling flagship and set a benchmark for the whiskey they will produce in the future. There is also a tasty grain whiskey and some Small Batch bottlings, but this is where I would start. Oh, and I would go and visit the distillery as well and see a real-life phoenix.

Colour Light mahogany.
Nose Bursting with fruity promise with peppery undertones.
Taste Dried fruit and citrus peels. Vanilla, spices and stewed fruits. Hints of red wine and light oak. It's layered, complex and intriguing.
Finish A sweet and balanced finish with harmonious wine notes and some toasted oak.

Verdict

93

Producer
Distillery
Visitor Centre
Availability
Price

Teerenpeli Distillery Co.
Teerenpeli, Lahti, Finland
Yes – in restaurant
Specialists
■■■■

www.teerenpelidistillery.com

Teerenpeli

10 Years Old

I was very happy to help launch this Finnish whisky in London in October 2015 at the Whisky Show (and, no, they weren't paying me), for two reasons: I have great admiration for the effort and dedication which have brought them this far and because I think it's a very decent whisky.

This is Finland's first real whisky to break out internationally and actually one of the very first small-scale craft distillers anywhere – as witness the fact that they can launch a 10 Years Old. Operations began in the basement cellar of Anssi Pyysing's Taivaanranta restaurant in the little Finnish town of Lahti.

Pyysing had previously pioneered an in-pub brewery, taking that on to greater things, and as a single malt enthusiast wanted to see if he could make whisky. The area is noted for barley production and high-quality water so he ordered stills and other equipment from Forsyths and hired an ex-Diageo Master Distiller to help set it up and train his team.

Being typically Finnish and determined to do a great job, nothing was released until the whisky was at least seven years old. Sufficient casks had been retained for this 10 Years Old and stocks have been held back for even older expressions.

Meanwhile the distillery has outgrown its original site. That will continue in operation and as the brand home, but a new plant has been commissioned on the edge of town, adjacent to the company's brewing operations. The new distillery mirrors the original but on a larger scale, meaning that Teerenpeli will be able to expand their range and increase international sales in future years.

This 10 Years Old pioneer is a great tribute to the creativity of the craft distilling movement and could happily be tasted against whiskies from distilleries with long and distinguished histories. Teerenpeli means 'flirtation' in Finnish – I can assure you that there is nothing frivolous about this lovely dram or the people who make it. So, we may safely conclude, *'Kauppa se on, joka kannattaa.'**

Colour Bright gold.

Nose Vanilla and honey.

Taste Rich, with cooked apples and custard dusted with pepper.

Finish Fades gently; very consistent.

Verdict

* 'It's trade that's profitable.' Finnish proverb.

Producer
Distillery
Visitor Centre
Availability
Price

Burn Stewart Distillers Ltd
Tobermory, Mull
Yes – tours by appointment
Specialists
■■

www.tobermorymalt.com

Tobermory

10 Years Old

There is something undeniably romantic about the idea of Tobermory distillery. For one thing, it's on an island. And for another, it's small and has battled for survival against all the odds – the distillery was founded in 1798 (Barnard says 1823), but was 'silent' for long periods in the mid 1800s and 1930s, twice revived during the 1970s, then under threat of property development until it came into the ownership of Burn Stewart in 1993. So it would be nice if it could succeed.

But the kindest thing that one could say about much of the whisky, marketed alternately as Tobermory and Ledaig (the peated style), is that the quality was variable. Frankly, to adapt the words of the rhyme, when it was good, it was just about OK; but when it was bad, it was horrid. I have had some shockers from this distillery. However, at last there's some good news.

The whisky coming through now has been distilled by deeply committed, long-term owners and, under the guidance of the traditionally minded Ian McMillan, Burn Stewart's former Master Blender and something of a zealot (in a good way), the quality of Tobermory is much improved. He has since moved on to mastermind the regeneration of Bladnoch but leaves an impressive legacy.

Sadly, stocks of the 15 Years Old, which I greatly liked, have been exhausted. The alternative is this 10 Years Old. Not perhaps as dark and brooding as its older brother, it offers a fresh and fruity introduction to the distillery, which is arguably now producing some of the best whisky in its long history. For a 46% abv bottle, aged 10 years, with some notable awards under its belt, it's currently something of a bargain at well under £40.

Burn Stewart's marketing team have also raised their game, with a nice bottle, handsome box and an interesting website. So, there you are – a good news story. Now try some!

Colour Pale gold.

Nose Light, fresh and floral but with some warehouse aromas.

Taste Honeyed, with smoke and ground pepper hints lingering in the background.

Finish Evolving spice adds some intrigue and complexity.

Verdict

95

Producer
Distillery
Visitor Centre

Availability
Price

William Grant & Sons
Tullamore, Tullamore, Co. Offaly
Yes – but in the town, no public
access to the distillery
Widespread
☐

www.tullamoredew.com

Tullamore D.E.W

First up, it's not 'dew', as in the drops of water condensed on the sweet grasses of an Irish meadow one gentle morning. Nothing so poetic. They're simply the initials of Daniel Edmund Williams who rose from stable boy to distillery owner, back in the day in duty-free outlets.

Of course much has changed since then. Irish whiskey has gone down in the world and then back up. In the course of that turbulent history the original Tullamore distillery was closed; the brand changed hands several times and today it's owned by William Grant & Sons, owners of Glenfiddich and The Balvenie.

Since acquiring the business in July 2010 they've been busy. The last surviving distillery building in Tullamore has been turned into a smart visitor centre, with shop and restaurant, and, more importantly, they have poured more than £30 million into a purpose-built state-of-the-art distillery, warehousing and a bottling complex just outside the town. It's hugely impressive. Sadly, they don't let the public inside, though I have a feeling they may just relent on that after a few years.

Tullamore D.E.W. itself is actually the bestselling Irish whiskey after Jameson, and number one in some Eastern European markets (Jameson dominates the hugely important US market). Grants didn't spend all this money for nothing though, and have ambitious long-term plans for the brand.

This is the entry-level version and is a perfectly pleasant, if undemanding, whiskey. But be honest – do you always want your whiskey making demands of you? Sometimes you just want to lift a glass with friends and not have to worry about, or discuss in serious tones, what's in that glass. And it's nice not to have to wince at the cost every time you pour another.

This could be the answer and, as a straightforward and approachable approach to Irish whiskey you can do worse. However, if you're a traveller, look out for the higher strength Phoenix with its greater weight and body.

Colour Pale gold.
Nose Fruits, some nuts, vanilla and red apples.
Taste Smooth mouthfeel. Buttered brioche and heather honey.
Finish Fades to toffee sweetness.

Verdict

96

Producer	WhistlePig
Distillery	WhistlePig, Shoreham, Vermont
Visitor Centre	No
Availability	Specialists
Price	▪▪▪▪

www.whistlepigwhiskey.com

WhistlePig
10 Year Old Rye

'Them good ole boys were drinking whiskey 'n' rye,' sang Don McLean back in 1971. And back in 1971 that *is* who was drinking rye; certainly not bearded hipsters with an armful of tattoos. In the years that followed, the good ole boys died off one by one and rye followed them all the way to the grave.

A few distilleries clung on, but the industry invested little or nothing in the product, packaging or promotion. Rye's demise seemed only a matter of time.

But a few contrary folk took a different view. Amongst them was Raj Peter Bhakta who purchased the WhistlePig Farm in rural Vermont and started to work with Master Distiller Dave Pickerell, formerly of Maker's Mark. Their goal: to transform WhistlePig Farm into the first ever single malt, one-stop rye shop, with all stages of the process located on site: from growing the grass, to distillation, to barrelling and aging, to bottling.

Well, that took some nerve but, to cut a long and tangled story short, they did it and today with the distillery finally open (but, sadly, closed to visitors) the last piece of the jigsaw is in place. Not quite, however, for now they have a new vision: to launch their own Vermont Estate Whiskey. This, they suggest, will rival the finest whiskeys in the world, and by 2020 their fully integrated single-estate rye aims to establish WhistlePig as the premier grain-to-glass distillery in America.

This 10 Years Old, pretty much their entry-level expression, was distilled and initially aged in Canada, before years of further aging in Vermont, creating some criticism for a perceived lack of transparency on its genesis. But once sampled, it met with rapturous acclaim because the world (and in particular bearded, hipster mixologists, especially the ones with tattoos) had started to cry out for rye – yes, for ten years it was on its own and then, by some miracle, the music played again.

Colour Warm amber
Nose Intense – fruity, spicy and spearmint.
Taste A sweet crumble base then cloves, nutmeg, cinnamon in glorious profusion.
Finish Nutty with toffee caramel and vanilla. And more spicy rye.

Verdict

97

Producer	Austin, Nichols Distilling Co. (Campari Group)
Distillery	Wild Turkey, Lawrenceburg, Kentucky
Visitor Centre	Yes
Availability	Specialists
Price	◼◼◼

www.wildturkeybourbon.com

Wild Turkey
Rare Breed

There are a number of Wild Turkey variants – a standard version at 8 years old; a number of aged versions; a rye; Russell's Reserve, named after legendary Master Distiller Jimmy Russell; and even a Honey Liqueur (with its own rather tacky 'American Honey' calendar, from a creative team that apparently eats regularly in Hooters and no doubt believes this is the epitome of upscale fine dining). All are good (with the possible exception of the calendar) but I suggest you seek out some Wild Turkey Rare Breed. It's a small-batch Kentucky Straight Bourbon Whiskey, blended from barrels at between 6 and 12 years of age and bottled at barrel strength (54.1% abv).

The distillery has been through several hands: most recently it was sold by Pernod Ricard to raise cash to pay for their Absolut vodka purchase. It now belongs to the Italian Campari Group (they also own Glen Grant in Scotland). At the time of writing, their plans for the brand are unclear but it would seem unlikely that they will introduce fundamental change to a well-loved bourbon icon, references to which appear regularly in popular culture. Tours are available at the distillery.

This higher-strength spirit can take the addition of some water to open up the more delicate aromas, but go carefully. It does not require significant dilution and may be best enjoyed as a sipping whiskey, for those long evenings of contemplation – unless, of course, raucous revelry is more to your taste. If you do take a moment to contemplate, read the small booklet that comes with the bottle and consider joining the Rare Breed Society. It's a marketing tool to help gather your contact information but, for a brief moment, it's fun to pretend that you are a member of a privileged elite 'who share Jimmy Russell's deep interest in bourbon making and tasting'. Yee hah!

Colour Warm red to amber.

Nose High strength evident initially, then berries and vanilla and toffee.

Taste Caramel, corn, liquorice, some citrus notes and fresh red apples.

Finish Highly complex and layered, with a final kick.

Verdict

98

Producer	Austin, Nichols Distilling Co.
Distillery	Wild Turkey, Lawrenceburg, Kentucky
Visitor Centre	Yes
Availability	Specialists
Price	▫▫

www.wildturkeybourbon.com

Wild Turkey
Rye

Once upon a time there was a Wild Turkey 101 Proof Rye. But that seems to have flown away, or whatever wild turkeys do, so we must content ourselves with this 81 Proof version (that's 41.5% abv in real money). And, speaking of money, this is a little bit of a bargain at under £35 a bottle.

One significant change to this book since the first edition has been the number of rye whiskies that now appear. That's partly driven by the new-found fashionability of this style; partly by availability (which is in turn partly a function of the fashionability) and partly because I have come to like it more and more and I want to share the love.

The regulations dictate that the mash bill (mix of cereals) has to contain at least 51 per cent rye before the spirit may be labelled 'rye whiskey' (the rest is usually maize and malted barley). But that can result in a rather tame product, which is not really what we're looking for and hardly representative of the best this versatile, but rather demanding, grain can do. The good news is that here the distiller uses around two-thirds rye, giving more of the distinctive spicy note that drinkers love. The barrels have been charred heavily, in what's known as an 'alligator' char, to bring out striking vanilla and more spice notes.

But the consensus of opinion is that this isn't a rye for drinking straight but finds its natural home in cocktails. This is as it should be, for if we look back in history, the truly great classic whiskey cocktails were made with rye, not bourbon or Scotch. So if you want an Old Fashioned or a Sazerac, rye is the place to start, even more so if a Manhattan is to your taste.

And don't forget that America's first president, George Washington, suppressor of the Whiskey Insurrection, was also a distiller and what he made at Mount Vernon was rye. If it was good enough for the President of the United States, what's holding you back?

Colour Bright copper.
Nose Subtly spicy caraway and fruity floral notes.
Taste Vanilla, plenty of spicy hits now, with sweet oranges and wood flavours.
Finish Pepper.

Verdict

99

Producer
Brown-Forman Corporation

Distillery
Woodford Reserve, Versailles, Kentucky

Visitor Centre
Yes

Availability
Specialists and some supermarkets

Price
☐☐

www.woodfordreserve.com

Woodford Reserve

Don't make the mistake of asking directions to Versailles in a European accent (as I once did). All you get from the locals are blank looks – it's 'Versales'! But when you get there some things at least will seem familiar – especially the still room.

And that's because the distinctive pot stills in which Woodford Reserve is distilled were manufactured in Rothes, Scotland, and shipped to Kentucky where a distiller from Scotland taught the locals how to use them.

Single-batch bourbon was, in essence, the US's answer to the phenomenon of single malt Scotch and an attempt to make bourbon, which had acquired a blue-collar image, chic once again. Well, it's worked and Woodford Reserve was one of the first to show that it could be done.

The parent company, Brown-Forman Corporation (who also own Jack Daniel's), invested around $14 million in restoring the old Labrot & Graham distillery which they had owned for 30 years from 1941. They sold it in 1971, bought it back in 1994, turned it into a showpiece, and rebranded it as Woodford Reserve in 2003.

At first the product closely resembled another B-F brand, Old Forester, but today it's a vatting of some column-still whiskey with the output of the L&G pot stills, made in small batches.

The distillery, which is on an unusual boutique scale for the USA, has a fine visitor centre. Great stress is laid on the limestone spring water, cypress fermentation vessels, small pot stills and stone warehouses. The result is a Kentucky classic.

Colour Dark honey.
Nose Vanilla sweetness, honey, fresh fruits and hints of chocolate.
Taste Rich and warming, with layers of mint, tobacco, leather and fruit. Smooth and full-bodied. Will seem sweet to the European palate.
Finish Smooth and warming; very consistent and balanced.

Verdict

100

Producer
BeamSuntory

Distillery
Yamazaki, near Osaka, Honshu Island, Japan

Visitor Centre
Yes – rated as one of the best in the world and it also has an excellent whisky museum

Availability
Specialists, some supermarkets stock younger ages

Price
■■■■

www.theyamazaki.jp

Yamazaki

12 Years Old

Look out, Scotland! Wake up!

There used to be an arrogance in Scotland about Japanese whisky, best summed up in a Scotch Whisky Association publication of 1951: 'The Japs came to this country years ago, copied our plant and even employed some of our Speyside personnel. They produced an imitation of Speyside Whisky which was not good although drinkable.'

Such patronising attitudes die hard and may be observed to this day. To those who hold them I say, 'Look at the British car industry – then be afraid, be very afraid.'

The fact is that the best Japanese whisky is very, very good and very, very Japanese. Yes, their restlessly innovative, quality-obsessed producers copied the best of Scottish practice, but then they adapted and improved it for Japanese conditions. As a result, Japanese whisky is collecting prizes, winning medals and growing fast. From a small base, admittedly, but it can't be ignored. In fact, whiskies like this should be celebrated and although prices have risen these are still whiskies to track down, open and enjoy.

The original Japanese malt distillery, Yamazaki was founded in 1923 at the site of a famous water source where three rivers converge. The distillery is often shrouded in mist and the warehouses sit sheltered by a bamboo forest. Japanese distillers don't swap 'fillings' for their blends with rivals so the stills at Yamazaki are all different in size and shape, permitting a bewildering range of styles to be produced.

Try any you can find. There are other Japanese whiskies listed here but this one is a favourite and a great introduction to a whole other world of whisky.

Colour Gold.
Nose Vanilla, cloves and panettone.
Taste Medium-bodied. Sweet, then spicy. Honey and lemon. Dried fruits. Wood.
Finish Dry and spicy.

Verdict

101

Producer	Nikka
Distillery	Yoichi, Hokkaido, Japan
Visitor Centre	Yes
Availability	Specialists
Price	■■■

www.nikka.com

Yoichi

Single Malt

Here's a fitting end to this exploration of 101 whiskies to try before you die.

The company that today we know as Nikka was founded in July 1934 when Masataka Taketsuru bought a large parcel of reclaimed land by the Yoichi River, a site he recognised as being ideal for producing whisky in a Scottish style. This had been his dream since studying distilling in Scotland from 1918–20 (during which time he also married Scots girl Rita Cowan). He returned to Japan in 1920 and helped establish the Yamazaki distillery.

But he wanted to build, own and operate his own 'Scottish' distillery in Japan and is widely honoured as the 'father' of Japanese whisky. Today Yoichi is owned by Asahi Breweries but continues to operate in a highly traditional manner, with direct-firing of the spirit stills and worm tubs for condensing the spirit. As elsewhere in Japan, the distillery can adapt quickly to differing styles of whisky, so no spirit from outside the company is required for blending.

Taketsuru managed the company through World War 2, its merger with Asahi and the development of the company's Sendai distillery in 1969. He eventually died in 1979, aged 85. In 1989 Nikka acquired the Ben Nevis distillery in Fort William, Scotland, and restarted production there, thus completing a kind of a circle in this remarkable man's contribution to the history and development of whisky in both Japan and Scotland.

There are several expressions available but the most accessible in the UK is this non-aged Single Malt (it used to be a 10 Years Old but the popularity of Japanese whiskies put paid to that). Various 'Nikka' branded malts are also seen, some of which contain whisky from Yoichi (e.g. Nikka Black and Nikka Taketsuru pure malts). Drink any of these and raise your glass to a true visionary and pioneer, who really tried before he died.

Colour Deep bronze.
Nose Bold and direct, with peat evident. Light citrus notes.
Taste Minty chocolate and orange oil. Creamy mouth feel and delicate peat smoke.
Finish Sweetness, peat and some antiseptic notes in alternate waves.

Verdict

How to taste whisky and use this book

Tasting whisky – any whisky – is straightforward. Follow these simple rules to get the most from your dram.

1. Use the right glass. A tumbler is hopeless. What you need is the Glencairn Crystal whisky glass (buy online from www.glencairn.co.uk). If you can't find those, get a sherry copita or brandy snifter to concentrate volatile aromas and help you 'nose' the whisky.

2. Fix the aroma and taste with associations – the smell of new-mown grass, for example, a vanilla-flavoured toffee or the rich taste of fruit cake.

3. Add a little water. It opens up the spirit and prevents your taste buds from becoming numbed by alcohol.

4. Roll the whisky right round your mouth and 'chew' it. Give the flavours time to develop: the whisky has been aging for years – give it as least as many seconds and the rewards will be huge.

5. Finally, think about the 'finish', or the lingering taste that remains. How consistent is it? What new flavours emerge?

Relax, keep practising and you'll very soon discover whisky's unique richness.

Imagine you were about to make a trip to a foreign land. Use this book as a sort of traveller's guide to the new country: it points you to some sights that you didn't know were there, or might otherwise have ignored on your journey. I don't claim to have all the answers; I don't know what whisky you like and there's no reason at all to assume that you'll like the same whiskies as me. That's why there are no scores here. But you can be assured that every whisky here is here for a reason and that they are good, often great, whiskies of their kind.

So try them at least once. Before you die.

Acknowledgements

My wife, Lindsay, has been enormously patient and put up with my grumpy moods and mental absences while writing this book. Presumably she's used to it by now. Worryingly, she claims that she didn't notice any difference. Either way, the biggest thanks go to her.

My agent, Judy Moir, believed in the book from the start and was positive, helpful and encouraging. Her husband, Neville, helped as well: he knows what he did! Thanks to both of them and to Bob McDevitt and Jonathan Taylor at Hachette for their enthusiasm and support. Jo Roberts-Miller – and Emma Tait for this third edition – did a great job editing the book in double-quick time.

I ruthlessly exploited most of my contacts in the wonderful world of whisky by asking them to nominate their three 'Desert Island Drams', without revealing the purpose of the enquiry. This group includes distillers, blenders, whisky writers, retailers, company directors and visitor centre guides – anyone, in fact, who seems to me to talk sense about whisky and was able and willing to offer some insights. The real reason, of course, was to ensure that I didn't miss anything out. Their cumulative wisdom drew my attention to many gems, but for this third edition I've gone solo!

In alphabetical order my 'oracles' were:
Russell Anderson, Raymond Armstrong, the late and greatly missed Helen Arthur, Dave Broom, Jonathan Brown, Chris Bunting, Frank Coleman, Yves Cosentino, Ronnie Cox, Jason Craig, Katherine Crisp, Jim Cryle, Kathleen Di Benedetto, Dr Clemens Dillmann, Duncan Elphick, Kevin Erskine, James Espey, Graham Eunson, Michael Fraser-Milne, John Glaser, Peter Gordon, Lawrence Graham, Alan Gray, Ken Grier, Teimei Horiuchi, Professor Paul Hughes, David Hume, Barrie Jackson, Richard Joynson, Naofumi Kamiguchi, Mike Keiller, Iain Kennedy, David King, John Lamond, Bill Lark, Jim Long, Mhairi MacDonald, Neil MacDonald, Ian MacIlwain, Charlie MacLean, Ian MacMillan, Nial Mackinlay, Anabel Meikle, Marcin Miller, Tatsuya Minagawa, Philip Morrice, Peter Muller, Peter Mulryan, David Nathan-Maister, Stuart Nickerson, Alex Nicol, Martine Nouet, Becky Offringa, Hans Offringa, Bill Owens, Richard Paterson, Brett Pontoni, Vijay Rekhi, Ken Robertson, Ingvar Ronde, Dominic Roskrow, Franz Scheurer, Colin Scott, Jacqui Seargeant, Sukhinder Singh, Gavin D. Smith, Stuart Smith, David Stewart, Steven Sturgeon, Jack Teeling, Luke Tegner, Jeffrey Topping, Misako Udo, Kerry Walsh Skerry, Iain Weir, Neil Wilson, Alan Winchester, David Wishart, Ian Wisniewski and Graham Wright.

My thanks to all of them.
The changes to this third edition are all my own work. Any mistakes are down to me alone.

Further resources

Books

There are many, many books and websites about whisky; some would say too many. However, I have suggested just a few here for further reading, the idea being (like the list of whiskies) to point you in various directions in the pursuit of knowledge.

The first modern book written about whisky was Aeneas MacDonald's *Whisky*. Despite its age (it first appeared in 1930), it is well worth reading as a poetic general introduction to Scotch whisky that is still surprisingly relevant. A new edition will appear shortly.

For the history of the Scotch whisky industry, Michael Moss and John Hume's *The Making of Scotch Whisky* is valuable, though dry and now somewhat dated. *Scotch Whisky – A Liquid History* by Charles Maclean is rather easier going. Any title by Charlie is worth reading.

Gavin D. Smith is very strong on the people and personalities in Scotch. Look out for *The Whisky Men*. For taste evaluation of Scotch whiskies, try *Whisky Classified* by David Wishart.

There is very little in English on Japanese whisky. Perhaps the most authoritative is *Japanese Whisky: Facts, Figures and Taste* by Ulf Buxrud. It does what it says in the title. Peter Mulyran's *The Whiskeys of Ireland* is the up-to-date account of Irish whiskey that we have badly needed and Fred Minnick and Lew Bryson both write authoratatively on US whiskies.

For more comprehensive coverage of all world whiskies and a basic introduction, look for *World Whisky* edited by Charles MacLean. I was one of a number of contributors. The new edition of the late Michael Jackson's *Malt Whisky Companion* has been compiled by Dominic Roskrow and Gavin Smith and is exhaustive. Some people find Jim Murray's annual *Whisky Bible* useful. He tastes almost everything!

The *Malt Whisky Yearbook* is issued annually and covers more than just single malt. It is an invaluable guide: accurate, regularly updated and a mine of interesting information, especially on new distilleries.

Magazines

There are various magazines. Perhaps the best (in English) are *Whisky Quarterly*, *Whisky Magazine* (UK, also a French edition) and their American counterpart *Whisky Advocate*. Dutch readers get *Whisky Etc.* and *Whisky Passion*.

Websites

There are literally hundreds, perhaps thousands, of websites on whisky, ranging from the exhaustive to the scanty, the authoritative and reliable to the frankly eccentric. Bloggers come and go and maintain their sites with different levels of enthusiasm and accuracy. Virtually every brand of note maintains its own site: if you read between the PR lines, there may be some useful information.

Given that the web evolves and changes both rapidly and constantly, the following recommendations may be of limited value. However, for what it is worth, I do look at these sites fairly regularly. Apologies to those that I have missed or forgotten about. A few hours of Googling will turn up more whisky sites than you thought possible. Good luck!

www.maltmadness.com
(set aside a good chunk of time if you venture here)

www.maltmaniacs.net
(I can't imagine how they find the time to keep this up!)

www.nonjatta.blogspot.com
(reports in English from Japan)

www.ralfy.com
(this is great fun)

www.thescotchblog.com
(one of the best-informed blogs

www.whiskycast.com
(authoritative whisky podcasts)

www.whiskyfun.com
('it's about single malts, music, enjoying life in general')

www.whisky-pages.com
(Gavin D. Smith's tasting notes and reviews)

Where to buy

There are now a great number of off-licences (liquor stores) all round the world that trade as whisky specialists, and many of them are excellent, with knowledgeable and enthusiastic staff. I can think of examples as far away as Switzerland, Singapore, New Zealand and, of course, the USA. New ones are springing up all the time as whisky grows in popularity and the choice they offer can be deliciously bewildering. In the interests of my sanity though, this section is restricted to the UK, where fortunately for us we are spoilt for choice with excellent specialist whisky retailers. The following have particularly good online shopping facilities:

Master of Malt
www.masterofmalt.com

Royal Mile Whiskies, Edinburgh
www.royalmilewhiskies.com

The Whisky Exchange, London
www.thewhiskyexchange.com

But ideally you should browse and talk to some enthusiastic and well-informed staff. There are many more good shops, notably The Whisky Shop (UK wide), The Wee Dram (Bakewell, Derbyshire), Lincoln Whisky Shop, The Whisky Shop (Dufftown), The Whisky Castle (Tomintoul), Arkwrights (Highworth, Wiltshire), Parkers of Banff, Robert Grahams (Glasgow), Whiskies of Scotland (Huntly), Nickolls & Perks (Stourbridge) and Luvians (St Andrews).

Above all, Gordon & MacPhail's shop in Elgin is a shrine and well worth a visit.

In London you will find The Whisky Exchange, Royal Mile Whiskies, Berry Bros & Rudd, Milroy's of Soho and The Vintage House. Nationally, the better Oddbins stores have a good selection of whisky and they have a good website, too.